Take Five:
Organizational
Behavior
Alive

Take Five:
Organizational Behavior Alive

JOSEPH E. CHAMPOUX

ARCHWAY
PUBLISHING

Archway Publishing books may be ordered through booksellers or by contacting:

Archway Publishing
1663 Liberty Drive
Bloomington, IN 47403
www.archwaypublishing.com
1 (888) 242-5904

From CHAMPOUX ICO. *Organizational Behavior* 1E. © 2001 South-Western, a part of
Cengage Learning, Inc. Reproduced by permission. www.cengage.com/permissions

ISBN: 978-1-4808-1526-1 (sc)
ISBN: 978-1-4808-1527-8 (e)

Library of Congress Control Number: 2015902890

Print information available on the last page.

Archway Publishing rev. date: 03/16/2015

To my grandchildren:
Blaise, Milo, Rémy, and Elektra.

Preface

Films offer a rich resource for learning organizational behavior theories, concepts, and issues. This resource of over a century of film making is readily available on DVDs. It ranges from such classics as *The Godfather* (1972) to contemporary films such as *Morning Glory* (2010). Animated films, which have enjoyed a renaissance with computer graphics technology, also offer organizational behavior learning resources. *James and the Giant Peach* (1996), for example, has a wonderful scene showing workforce diversity.

This book is the product of my on-going cinema-based research and cinema-based teaching. I have found that students respond positively to the link between film scenes and abstract theories and concepts. Film offers a visualization of organizational behavior concepts that often are abstract in textbooks and lectures. For example, one can read about ethical dilemmas. A visualization of ethical dilemmas with a carefully chosen film scene can reinforce it dramatically. *Grumpier Old Men* (1995) has a closing scene showing ethical dilemmas. John (Jack Lemmon) and Max (Walter Matthau) must decide whether to go to Max's wedding or try, once again, to catch the most elusive fish in the lake, "Catfish Hunter."

I have carefully viewed and selected film scenes that show organizational behavior concepts and issues. This book will work well as a supplement for organizational behavior courses at the undergraduate, graduate, and executive levels. The chapter order is about the same as most popular organizational behavior textbooks. This order should let you and your instructor easily align the film scenes and their themes with your course's main text.

Each chapter has four scenes drawn from four different feature films. Chapters start with an introduction to the chapter's concept, theory, or issue.[1] The chapter then discusses each film scene in a convenient two-page format. The left page describes the film and the scene; the right page has space for your analysis and personal reactions. If a film's title includes a Roman numeral, the book discusses the film again with a different concept, theory, or issue.

Each scene discussion includes film and scene descriptions, and a list of questions and issues to think about and watch for while viewing the scene. There is also a list of Concepts or Examples. If these Concepts or Examples appear in the scene, you can check them off when you see them. Marking them as you see them helps you write your analysis.

I provide scene starting and stopping points so you can quickly find the scene on the referenced DVD. I also give approximate scene running times to help you manage your classroom and independent study time. These estimates are specific to the distributor's DVD shown under the film title.

Scene descriptions in this book have enough detail to let you locate the scene on a DVD. The descriptions use a "bracketing" technique, describing what occurs before and after the

---

[1]   I adapted the chapter introductions from material in Joseph E. Champoux, *Organizational Behavior: Integrating Individuals, Groups, and Organizations*, 4e, New York: Routledge, 2011.

scene. This method will help you find the scene quickly, especially if you are unfamiliar with the film.

You can use this book in different ways. Your instructor might show the scene in class for class discussion. He or she may ask you to write an analysis in class in the space provided and turn it in at a designated time. Or, your instructor might assign scenes for your out-of-class viewing as an individual or in small groups. He or she may want you to write your analysis and turn it in for class credit.

You can also use film scenes in this book for individual or group presentations in other classes. For example, the problem-solving and decision-making scenes in Chapters 19 and 20 would work well in presentations for an Operations Management class. Using film scenes in such presentations can enliven them and help you make your points effectively.

This book also works well for independent study. You can supplement your reading and other studying by viewing scenes linked to topics you are trying to learn.

I based the film descriptions in this book on the latest versions of the following film reference sources:

- *Leonard Maltin's Movie Guide*
- *The Seventh Virgin Film Guide*
- *VideoHound's Golden Movie Retriever*

I also used the Internet Movie Database (http://www.imdb.com) and different film studies resources referenced in various chapters.

You may enjoy learning more about a specific film. I suggest using the reference books mentioned and the Internet Movie Database. This site has news about new and older films and lets you search for specific film information.

I have used the film scenes described in this book in my undergraduate, Masters of Business Administration (MBA), and Executive MBA classes for many years. I also have used many scenes in classes that I have taught in countries outside the United States. As a result, students and colleagues have recommended many scenes in this book for which they receive recognition. To all of you, I extend my greatest thanks for your positive responses and continual support.

An effort such as this Student Workbook is always a "work-in-progress." I would enjoy feedback about any aspect of its content and design. Please send your comments and observations to me at 10201 Modesto Avenue NE, Albuquerque, New Mexico, 87122-3906 USA. You can also send email to champoux@unm.edu.

Joseph E. Champoux, PhD
Albuquerque, New Mexico, USA

Contents

CHAPTER 1

Introduction to Organizations and Management

An **organization** is a system of two or more persons, engaged in cooperative action, trying to reach a purpose.[2] Organizations are bounded systems of structured social interaction featuring authority relations, communication systems, and the use of incentives. Examples of organizations include businesses, hospitals, colleges, retail stores, and prisons.[3]

We are all part of organizations, whether we want to be or not. You are now part of an organization—your college, university, or employing organization. In your daily round of activities, you move from one organization to another. You may shop at a store, deal with a government agency, or go to work. Understanding organizations and their management can give you significant insights into systems that have major effects on you.

The scenes discussed in this chapter come from the following films:

- *Antz*
- *Brazil*
- *Catch-22*
- *The Secret of My Success*

Antz offers an animated symbolic rendering of the world of work. *Brazil* gives a comic, satiric view of bureaucracies. *Catch-22* describes the now famous "catch," which shows that managers build policies into their organizations with little prior knowledge of their effects. *The Secret of My Success* shows the first-day-at-work experiences of a newly hired college graduate.

---

2   Chester I. Barnard, *The Functions of the Executive* (Cambridge: Harvard University Press, 1938), 73.
3   Peter M. Blau and W. Richard Scott, *Formal Organizations: A Comparative Approach* (San Francisco: Chandler Publishing Co., 1962); Amitai Etzioni, *Modern Organizations* (Englewood Cliffs, NJ: Prentice Hall, 1964); W. Richard Scott, "Theory of Organizations," in *Handbook of Modern Sociology*, ed. Robert E. L. Faris (Chicago: Rand McNally, 1964), 485–529.

Antz (I)

Color, 1998
Running Time: 1 hour, 23 minutes
Rating: PG
Director: Eric Darnell, Tim Johnson
Distributor: DreamWorks Home Entertainment

Z (voiced by Woody Allen) is an insignificant worker ant in a massive ant colony. He is trying to find his role in life and pursue Princess Bala (voiced by Sharon Stone). Everything changes after he trades places with his soldier ant friend Weaver (voiced by Sylvester Stallone). A termite war and the pursuit of the evil General Mandible (voiced by Gene Hackman) take Z's life to new and unexpected places. It helps us imagine our world, organizations, and ourselves from the perspective of some wonderfully animated insect creatures.[4]

Note: Chapter 7 "Perception" discusses other scenes from this film.

SCENES

DVD CHAPTER 1. INSIGNIFICANTZ (MAIN TITLES) TO CHAPTER 2. THE GENERAL'S PLAN (0:00:49–0:08:00)

These scenes start after the opening credits with a shot of the New York City skyline. Z's voice-over says, "All my life I've lived and worked in the big city." They end as General Mandible and Colonel Cutter (voiced by Christopher Walken) leave to meet the queen. Mandible says, "Our very next stop, Cutter." The film cuts to the meeting between the Queen (voiced by Anne Bancroft) and General Mandible.

WHAT TO WATCH FOR AND ASK YOURSELF

- What major work-related issues do these scenes raise?
- Do you see these issues in your work experiences?
- What is your preferred "world of work?"

---

[4] Originally suggested by Greg McNeil, undergraduate student, The Robert O. Anderson School of Management, The University of New Mexico.
Joseph E. Champoux, "Animated Films as a Teaching Resource," *Journal of Management Education* 25, no. 1 (2001): 78–99. *Note:* Portions of this article used in this chapter with permission.
From CHAMPOUX ICO. *Organizational Behavior*, 1e. © 2001 South-Western, a part of Cengage Learning, Inc. Reproduced by permission. www.cengage.com/permissions

CONCEPTS OR EXAMPLES

☐ Personal needs

☐ Worker contribution to the larger organization

☐ Meaningful work

☐ Theory X assumptions

☐ Supervisory behavior

☐ Theory Y assumptions

ANALYSIS

_____

_____

_____

_____

_____

_____

_____

_____

_____

PERSONAL REACTIONS

_____

_____

_____

_____

_____

_____

_____

_____

_____

_____

Brazil

Color, 1985
Running Time: 2 hours, 11 minutes
Rating: R
Director: Terry Gilliam
Distributor: Universal Home Video, Inc.

This film is a surrealistic, comedic look at a fictitious future world dominated by massive bureaucracies. Directed by former Monty Python member Terry Gilliam, the film follows bureaucrat Sam Lowry (Jonathan Pryce) in his search for the beautiful, mysterious Jill Layton (Kim Greist). The engaging photography, music, and film editing help show this future society's oppressive bureaucracy.

SCENES

Two sets of scenes introduce you to the Ministry of Information and show how it functions. They each show different aspects of behavior in organizations.

DVD CHAPTER 1 SOMEWHERE IN THE 20ᵀᴴ CENTURY TO CHAPTER 3 WHERE'S SAM LOWRY? (0:00:23–0:09:52)

The first scenes start at the beginning of the film with a shot of clouds, after some opening credits. The 1930 Ary Borroso's song "Brazil" plays in the background.[5] They end after Mr. Kurtzman (Ian Holm) asks whether anyone has seen Sam Lowry. The film cuts to another cloud shot. This begins Sam Lowry's dream of flying toward a beautiful, mysterious woman, whom he discovers at the Ministry in the second set of scenes.

DVD CHAPTER 4 THE MINISTRY OF INFORMATION (0:12:23–0:15:39)

The second set of scenes, which follow the scene of Sam Lowry preparing to go to work, start with a panning shot of the Ministry of Information's giant icon. They end after Jill pushes the surveillance machine out of her way and storms out of the Ministry. The film cuts to a sign reading, "Suspicion Breeds Confidence." Sam works with a computer at Mr. Kurtzman's desk while Kurtzman looks over his shoulder.

WHAT TO WATCH FOR AND ASK YOURSELF

- What type of organizational behavior do these scenes show?
- Are there any manifest functions of this behavior?
- Are there any latent dysfunctions of the same behavior?

---

[5] Didier C. Deutsch, ed., *VideoHound's Soundtracks: Music from the Movies, broadway and television* (Detroit, MI: Visible Ink Press, 1998), 60–61.

CONCEPTS OR EXAMPLES

- ☐ Organization
- ☐ Organizational behavior

- ☐ Bureaucracy
- ☐ Bureausis, bureautic (intolerance of bureaucratic behavior)
- ☐ Manifest functions (intended positive results)

- ☐ Bureaucratic behavior
- ☐ Bureaupathology (excessive bureaucratic behavior)
- ☐ Means-ends inversion
- ☐ Latent dysfunctions (unintended negative results)

ANALYSIS

_____

_____

_____

_____

_____

_____

_____

PERSONAL REACTIONS

_____

_____

_____

_____

_____

_____

_____

_____

_____

Catch-22

Color, 1970
Running Time: 2 hours, 1 minute
Rating: R
Director: Mike Nichols
Distributor: Paramount Pictures

Army Air Corps officers are bone weary from flying too many missions during World War II. This black comedy satire pokes fun at military life and shows the stress of war. Captain Yossarian (Alan Arkin) makes endless efforts to not fly any more missions. He discovers a "catch" to his efforts to be grounded because of insanity. Anyone who flies combat missions must be insane; anyone who asks to be grounded must be sane!

SCENES

DVD CHAPTER 2. PERSECUTION COMPLEX (0:08:39–0:11:06)

These scenes start with a close-up of Flight Surgeon Doc Daneeka's (Jack Guilford) face as he says, "There's nothing wrong with it." Yossarian replies, "Well look at it once." This sequence follows the dining hall discussion about Yossarian's persecution feelings. It ends as Doc appears upside down while saying, "It's the best there is." The film cuts to Major Danby (Richard Benjamin) talking to the flight crews about the day's mission.

WHAT TO WATCH FOR AND ASK YOURSELF

- Are there examples of excessive bureaucratic behavior (bureaupathology) in these scenes?
- If so, what specific behaviors do you see?
- Have you had any experiences similar to those shown in the scenes?

CONCEPTS OR EXAMPLES

☐ Bureaucratic behavior

☐ Bureaupathology (excessive bureaucratic behavior, dysfunctional bureaucracy)

☐ Functional behavior

☐ Bureausis, bureautic (intolerance of bureaucracy)

☐ Rules, policies, procedures

☐ Means-ends inversion

☐ Dysfunctional behavior

ANALYSIS

_____

_____

_____

_____

_____

_____

_____

_____

PERSONAL REACTIONS

_____

_____

_____

_____

_____

_____

_____

_____

_____

The Secret of My Success

Color, 1987
Running Time: 1 hour, 50 minutes
Rating: PG-13
Director: Herbert Ross
Distributor: Universal Home Video, Inc.

This film is an entertaining look at corporate life featuring power, negotiation, and sexual shenanigans. It begins when college graduate Brantley Foster (Michael J. Fox) leaves his Kansas home and goes to New York City. He wants to succeed as an executive but can only land a mailroom job. By impersonating an executive, and frantically balancing his mailroom and executive jobs, he hopes to impress the beautiful Christy Wills (Helen Slater).

SCENES

DVD CHAPTER 4. THE NEW JOB (0:17:42–0:20:49)

The scenes start with a shot of the mailroom and Brantley Foster arriving for his first workday. They follow Brantley's exhausting job search and the first time he sees Christy. These scenes end after the lunch conversation on the street with coworker Fred Melrose (John Pankow). The film cuts to Brantley talking to a Research Department clerk (Mary Catherine Wright).

WHAT TO WATCH FOR AND ASK YOURSELF

- What do these scenes suggest you will learn on your first day on the job?
- From whom does Brantley learn his job's key features?
- Is there any evidence of status differences in this company?

CONCEPTS OR EXAMPLES

☐ Required work behavior   ☐ Social status

☐ Jargon   ☐ Status relationships

☐ Social relationships

ANALYSIS

_____

_____

_____

_____

_____

_____

_____

_____

_____

PERSONAL REACTIONS

_____

_____

_____

_____

_____

_____

_____

_____

_____

_____

_____

CHAPTER 2
Workforce Diversity

Workforce diversity refers to variations in workforce composition based on personal and background factors of employees or potential employees. Those factors include age, gender, race, ethnicity, physical ability, and sexual orientation. Other factors focus on family status, such as a single parent, a dual-career relationship, or a person with responsibilities for aging parents.[6]

Bureau of Labor Statistics' projections[7] show the twenty-first century's workforce as having more female and minority workers than in earlier years. Age diversity will also continue with almost 26 percent of the labor force at age 55 or over in 2022. The expected labor force gender and ethnic profile shows 47 percent women and 22 percent minority workers.

People from different social backgrounds, cultures, and language groups bring different world views to an organization.[8] They view work issues and problems through different perceptual lenses. If properly managed, these different views present opportunities to organizations, but they also increase an organization's conflict potential.

The scenes showing aspects of diversity come from the following films:

- *Babe*
- *Brassed Off!*
- *James and the Giant Peach*
- *Young Frankenstein*

The scenes from *Babe* show how hard it is for a person (in this case, a young pig) to change basic characteristics. *Brassed Off!*, a British film, shows grudging acceptance of a woman into an all-male brass band. *James and the Giant Peach* is an eye-popping, stop-motion animated film with a striking diversity scene. *Young Frankenstein* is a delightful portrayal of the acceptance of differences in the famous blind hermit scene with Gene Hackman and Peter Boyle.

---

[6] V. Robert Hayles and Amida M. Russell, *The Diversity Directive: Why Some Initiatives Fail & What to Do About It* (Chicago: Irwin Professional Publishing, 1997); Susan E. Jackson and Associates, eds. *Diversity in the Workplace: Human Resources Initiatives* (New York: Guilford Press, 1992); David Jamieson and Julie O'Mara, *Managing Workforce 2000: Gaining the Diversity Advantage* (San Francisco: Jossey-Bass, 1991).

[7] Mitra Toossi, "Labor force projections to 2022: the labor force participation rate continues to fall," *Monthly Labor Review* 136, no. 12 (2013): 1–28.

[8] Meg A. Bond and Jean L. Pyle, "The Ecology of Diversity in Organizational Settings: Lessons from a Case Study," *Human Relations* 51, no. 5 (1998): 589–623.

Babe

Color, 1995
Running Time: 1 hour, 32 minutes
Rating: G
Director: Chris Noonan
Distributor: Universal Studios

A charming Australian film featuring eccentric, quiet Farmer Hoggett (James Cromwell) who trains a pig he won at the fair to herd his sheep. His eccentricity turns to determination when he enters the pig in the Australian National Sheepdog Championships. The Academy Award-winning visual effects include a seamless mixture of animatronic doubles, computer images, and live animals.[9]

SCENES

DVD CHAPTER 8 A PIG THAT THINKS IT'S A DOG (0:38:18–0:44:35)

The scenes start with Farmer Hoggett opening his new motor-powered gate and calling his dogs and Babe. Hoggett says, "Come Rex. Come Fly. Come Pig." They follow the scene of Hoggett noticing that Babe sorted some chickens by color. These scenes end as Farmer Hoggett's horse-drawn wagon goes down a hill. Fly (voiced by Miriam Margolyes) says to Babe (voiced by Christine Cavanaugh), "No, no, no. I think you better leave that to me." The film cuts to a shot of the moon. The sheep call the dogs "wolves."

WHAT TO WATCH FOR AND ASK YOURSELF

- Are Babe's methods of herding sheep different from those used by sheepdogs? If *yes*, what are the differences?
- Does Babe discover that he cannot successfully herd sheep as a sheep dog herds them? What does he do?
- Does Farmer Hoggett accept Babe for what he is—a pig not a sheep dog?

---

[9] Champoux, "Animated Films," 79–100.

CONCEPTS OR EXAMPLES

- ☐ Diversity
- ☐ Different behaviors reach the same goal
- ☐ Cannot change who you are
- ☐ Dimensions of diversity
- ☐ Rejection of differences

- ☐ Managing diversity
- ☐ Valuing diversity
- ☐ Increased conflict potential
- ☐ Diversity and performance
- ☐ Acceptance of differences

ANALYSIS

_____

_____

_____

_____

_____

_____

_____

_____

PERSONAL REACTIONS

_____

_____

_____

_____

_____

_____

_____

_____

_____

_____

Brassed Off!

Color, 1996
Running Time: 1 hour, 41 minutes
Rating: R
Director: Mark Herman
Distributor: Buena Vista Home Entertainment

A touching story about the economic woes of Grimly, a fictional coal mining town in Yorkshire, England. The town faces the closing of its mine, a major source of employment. Playing in the mine's brass band is the only source of hope for many workers. Gloria Mullins (Tara Fitzgerald) arrives and becomes the band's first female player. Charming performances and great music soften the story's sadness. The Grimethorpe Colliery Brass Band plays the brass band music.[10] "Brassed off" is British slang for dejected or upset.

SCENES

DVD CHAPTER 3. BAND PRACTICE (0:11:08–0:21:22)

These scenes open with Danny (Pete Postlethwaite) and his son Phil (Stephen Thompkinson) riding Danny's bicycle to the rehearsal site. This sequence includes intercut scenes of union-management negotiations at the mine's office. The scenes end after Gloria says, "If I'm allowed." Danny says, "Don't be soft [silly], lass. You were born here." The screen goes black and the film cuts to a neighborhood scene.

WHAT TO WATCH FOR AND ASK YOURSELF

- Do the band members openly accept Gloria from the beginning?
- What persuades them that she can become an acceptable member?
- Do you expect her presence to help the band in its later competition?

---

[10] Joseph E. Champoux, "Seeing and Valuing Diversity Through Film," *Educational Media International* 36, no. 4 (1999): 310–16; Deutsch, *VideoHound's Soundtracks*, 60.

CONCEPTS OR EXAMPLES

- ☐ Workforce diversity
- ☐ Gender-based diversity
- ☐ Homogeneous group
- ☐ Heterogeneous group
- ☐ Diversity and performance

ANALYSIS

_____

_____

_____

_____

_____

_____

_____

_____

_____

PERSONAL REACTIONS

_____

_____

_____

_____

_____

_____

_____

_____

_____

_____

James and the Giant Peach (I)

Color, 1996
Running Time: 1 hour, 19 minutes
Rating: G
Director: Henry Selick
Distributor: Hollywood Pictures Home Video[11]

This captivating stop-motion animated film follows a young boy's quest to leave his awful aunts and go to New York City. He discovers a giant peach on a tree in his yard. James (voiced by Paul Terry) enters it and becomes part of the diverse world of Grasshopper (voiced by Simon Callow), Centipede (voiced by Richard Dreyfuss), Ladybug (voiced by Jane Leeves), Glowworm (voiced by Miriam Margolyes), Spider (voiced by Susan Sarandon), and Earthworm (voiced by David Thewlis). This film is brilliantly animated with a captivating though bizarre story.

Note: Chapter 19 "Problem Solving" also discusses scenes from this film.

SCENES

DVD CHAPTER 6. A LITTLE LEFTOVER MAGIC THROUGH CHAPTER 7. *"THAT'S THE LIFE"* (0:17:43–0:24:08)

This sequence follows the arrival of the giant peach and James' aunts' presentation of it to the public as a curiosity. They have just finished counting their proceeds from the presentation. James walks around the side of a sign, picking up trash with his pick. The sequence ends after Centipede climbs the ladder while saying, "Hup! Time to go make a pest of myself. Heh Heh!" The film cuts to Aunt Spiker (Joanna Limley) and Aunt Sponge (Miriam Margolyes) searching for him in the yard.

WHAT TO WATCH FOR AND ASK YOURSELF

- What dimensions of diversity appear in this sequence?
- What would you predict for this group working together?
- Would you expect conflict within the group because of their extreme differences?

---

[11] Buena Vista Home Entertainment and Walt Disney Studios Home Entertainment also distribute this film.

Joseph E. Champoux

CONCEPTS OR EXAMPLES

☐ Workforce diversity
☐ Heterogeneous group
☐ Homogeneous group
☐ Conflict potential

☐ Group performance
☐ Intragroup conflict
☐ Dimensions of diversity

ANALYSIS

_____

_____

_____

_____

_____

_____

_____

_____

_____

_____

PERSONAL REACTIONS

_____

_____

_____

_____

_____

_____

_____

_____

_____

_____

Young Frankenstein

Black and White, 1974
Running Time: 1 hour, 42 minutes
Rating: PG-13
Director: Mel Brooks
Distributor: Twentieth Century Fox Home Entertainment

Young Dr. Frederick Frankenstein (properly pronounced "FRONK-en-steen") (Gene Wilder) works in his grandfather's laboratory with the help of loony assistant Igor (properly pronounced "eye-gore") (Marty Feldman). This hilarious film spoofs the 1930s Frankenstein films. Dr. Frankenstein succeeds in creating The Monster (Peter Boyle) who seeks acceptance and affection but has a hard time finding it. Director Mel Brooks used the original laboratory props from the 1931 *Frankenstein* to make this film.[12] *Film trivia question:* Does Igor's hunchback change positions during the film?

SCENES

DVD CHAPTER 18. THE BLIND HERMIT (1:06:30–1:11:11)

The camera zooms to a house and goes to a lighted candle on a table. Harold The Blindman (Gene Hackman) is praying. These scenes follow Helga's (Anne Beesley) interaction with The Monster on a seesaw. He sits on it and throws her into her bedroom. The film sequence ends after The Monster leaves with his finger on fire. Harold says, "Wait! Wait! Where are you going? I was going to make espresso." The screen goes black. These scenes are a parody of a similar sequence in the 1935 *The Bride of Frankenstein*.[13]

WHAT TO WATCH FOR AND ASK YOURSELF

- Does this film sequence show acceptance of people's differences?
- What are the functional and dysfunctional results of such acceptance?
- Is there any evidence of stereotyping in these scenes?

---

[12] Champoux, "Seeing and Valuing Diversity," 310–16; Ken Fox, Ed Grant, and Jo Imeson, *The Seventh Virgin Film Guide* (London: Virgin Books, 1998); Leonard Maltin, ed., *Leonard Maltin's Movie Guide, 2015 Edition: The Modern Era* (New York: SIGNET, 2014): 1602.
[13] Maltin, *Maltin's Movie Guide*, 1602.

CONCEPTS OR EXAMPLES

☐ Perception   ☐ Stereotyping

☐ Diversity   ☐ Dimensions of diversity

☐ Acceptance of differences   ☐ Valuing diversity

ANALYSIS

_____

_____

_____

_____

_____

_____

_____

_____

_____

_____

PERSONAL REACTIONS

_____

_____

_____

_____

_____

_____

_____

_____

_____

CHAPTER 3
Quality Management

A major thrust of American management is the quality of products and services.[14] Although quality management can be traced to the 1920s,[15] American organizations did not embrace it until the early 1980s.[16] Quality management has many names including total quality control, total quality management, total quality leadership, leadership through quality, market driven quality, and Six Sigma quality. **Quality Management (QM)** is a philosophy and system of management that includes tools and techniques that help organizations manage for quality in services, products, and processes. Although its roots are in manufacturing, QM is a management system that can bring major improvements to any organization.

QM emphasizes a long-term commitment to continuous quality improvement. It stresses that quality is everyone's job, not only the job of a quality-control department. QM is intensely customer focused and demands that all organization members share that focus.[17] It emphasizes high work process involvement and communication in all directions: top-down, bottom-up, and laterally. This feature follows directly from the need for cooperation and high involvement.

Scenes from these films help show QM's customer focus:

- *Five Easy Pieces*
- *The Hospital*
- *Breakfast at Tiffany's*
- *Never Give a Sucker an Even Break*

---

[14] Joseph E. Champoux, "Management Context of Not-for-Profit Organizations in the Next Millennium: Diversity, Quality, Technology, Global Environment, and Ethics," in *The Nonprofit Management Handbook*. 2d ed. 1999 supplement, ed. Tracy D. Connors (New York: John Wiley & Sons), 7–9. *Note:* Parts of the chapter's introduction adapted from this essay. Copyright © 1999 by John Wiley & Sons, Inc. Reprinted by permission of John Wiley & Sons, Inc.

[15] G. S. Radford, *The Control of Quality in Manufacturing* (New York: The Ronald Press Company, 1922).

[16] David A. Garvin, *Managing Quality: The Strategic and Competitive Edge* (New York: Free Press, 1988); R. Ray Gehani, "Quality Value-Chain: A Meta-Synthesis of Frontiers of Quality Movement," *Academy of Management Executive* 7, no. 2 (1993): 29–42.

[17] Cynthia A. Lengnick-Hall, "Customer Contributions to Quality: A Different View of the Customer-Oriented Firm," *Academy of Management Review* 21, no. 3 (1996): 791–824.

Jack Nicholson's classic chicken salad sandwich scenes in *Five Easy Pieces* show the meaning of no customer service. The scenes from *The Hospital* show an insensitive insurance clerk's behavior. *Breakfast at Tiffany's* has an opposite sequence in which a Tiffany's sales clerk tries to satisfy Holly Golightly's (Audrey Hepburn) desire to stay within her budget. W. C. Fields plays The Great Man, an irritable restaurant customer, in *Never Give a Sucker an Even Break*.

Five Easy Pieces

Color, 1970
Running Time: 1 hour, 38 minutes
Rating: R
Director: Bob Rafelson
Distributor: The Criterion Collection

A young Jack Nicholson richly portrays Robert Eroica Dupea, a brilliant classical pianist who gives up his career to work in the oil fields. He is trying to return home to pay his last wishes to his dying father. Along the way, he picks up some female hitchhikers who each are character studies. They stop at a roadside restaurant for food where the classic chicken salad sandwich scene unfolds.[18]

SCENES

DVD CHAPTER 15 NO SUBSTITUTIONS (0:45:11–STOP: 0:47:05)

This sequence follows the hostile interactions in the car between Dupea's girlfriend Rayette (Karen Black) and hitchhiker Palm Apodaca (Helena Kallianiotes). The scenes start as Dupea orders his food from the waitress (Lorna Thayer). He says, "I'd like a plain omelet. Ah, no potatoes. Tomatoes instead. A cup of coffee and wheat toast." The film sequence ends with the group driving away from the restaurant. Palm Apodaca says, "No, but it was very clever. I would have just punched her out." The film cuts to a highway shot of their car going past some railroad tracks.

WHAT TO WATCH FOR AND ASK YOURSELF

- What do these scenes show about customer service?
- Is Robert Dupea an unreasonable customer?
- Is the waitress flexible or inflexible in her customer focus?

---

[18]   Jim Craddock, ed., *VideoHound's Golden Movie Retriever* (Farmington Hills, MI: Gale, Cengage Learning, 2014), 380.

CONCEPTS OR EXAMPLES

- ☐ Customer service (or absence)
- ☐ Quality management
- ☐ Customer focus (or absence)
- ☐ Flexible policies
- ☐ Inflexible policies

ANALYSIS

_____

_____

_____

_____

_____

_____

_____

_____

_____

_____

PERSONAL REACTIONS

_____

_____

_____

_____

_____

_____

_____

_____

_____

_____

The Hospital

Color, 1971
Running Time: 1 hour, 42 minutes
Rating: PG
Director: Arthur Hiller
Distributor: MGM Home Entertainment

A caustic, dark, satirical look at a big city hospital's inner workings. George C. Scott gives a suitably hammy performance from Paddy Chayefsky's Oscar winning screenplay. The film's many laughs will distract you from the drama of staff member deaths, odd relationships among hospital staff and patients, and bad medical care delivery.

SCENES

DVD CHAPTER 4. CPA VS. MD IN THE ER (0:22:27–0:25:51)

These scenes start in the emergency room with Sally (Frances Sternhagen) from accounting asking for Mr. Hemmings. She also asks other patients in the area about their health insurance. The sequence follows Dr. Herbert Bock's (George C. Scott) meeting for the residents' presentations. It ends after Dr. Spezio (Rehn Scofield) says the patient in the holding area is dead. The film cuts to a staff meeting with the staff eating sack lunches.

WHAT TO WATCH FOR AND ASK YOURSELF

- Do these scenes show the presence or absence of a customer focus?
- Would a customer focus view of Sally's role in accounting better serve the hospital? Why or why not?
- What other unintended dysfunctions do these scenes show?

CONCEPTS OR EXAMPLES

- ☐ Customer focus (or absence)
- ☐ Quality management
- ☐ Bureaupathology (excessive bureaucratic behavior)

- ☐ Customer needs or desires
- ☐ Bureaucracy
- ☐ Bureaucratic behavior

ANALYSIS

_____

_____

_____

_____

_____

_____

_____

_____

_____

PERSONAL REACTIONS

_____

_____

_____

_____

_____

_____

_____

_____

_____

_____

Breakfast at Tiffany's

Color, 1961
Running Time: 1 hour, 54 minutes
Rating: NR
Director: Blake Edwards
Distributor: Paramount Home Video

*A*n endearing Truman Capote story about Holly Golightly (Audrey Hepburn), a young rural woman who becomes a New York playgirl. She has a shaky romance with writer Paul Varjak (George Peppard). Although now almost a period film of mid-20th century New York life, the comedy and charming romance come through for any audience. The film features Henry Mancini's Academy Award winning song, "Moon River." In 2002, the American Film Institute ranked *Breakfast at Tiffany's* among the top 100 cinema love stories.[19]

SCENES

DVD CHAPTER 10. THINGS WE'VE NEVER DONE (1:08:03–1:12:54)

These scenes start with Paul and Holly walking along a Manhattan street. They follow the scene of Paul opening champagne in Holly's apartment. The sequence ends after Holly kisses the Tiffany's salesman (John MacGiver) and says, "Didn't I tell you this is a lovely place." The film dissolves to Paul and Holly looking into a store window. They continue their Manhattan stroll and go to the public library so Holly can sit and rest.[20]

WHAT TO WATCH FOR AND ASK YOURSELF

- Does the Tiffany's salesman focus on the needs and desires of Paul and Holly?
- Is he flexible in his response to their request? What does he do to meet their budget requirements?
- Would you expect this type of customer service in a modern, upscale jewelry store?

---

[19] D. Germain, "'Casablanca' Top Romance Film: Institute Picks 100 Best Love Stories," *The Associated Press*. As the story appeared in the *Albuquerque Journal*. (June 12, 2002), C13.

[20] Originally suggested by Elizabeth McCormick, Olivia Timmons, and Jeff Loafman, undergraduate students, The Robert O. Anderson School of Management, The University of New Mexico.

CONCEPTS OR EXAMPLES

☐ Quality management   ☐ Flexible response

☐ Customer service   ☐ Inflexible response

☐ Customer focus

ANALYSIS

_____

_____

_____

_____

_____

_____

_____

_____

_____

_____

_____

PERSONAL REACTIONS

_____

_____

_____

_____

_____

_____

_____

_____

_____

_____

_____

Never Give a Sucker an Even Break

Black and White, 1941
Running Time: 1 hour, 11 minutes
Rating: NR
Director: Edward F. Cline
Distributor: Universal Home Entertainment

The legendary comedian W. C. Fields–in his last starring role–plays himself, The Great Man. This caustic spoof of Hollywood film production let Fields take his last shots before Universal Studios replaced him as their lead comic with Abbott and Costello. No real plot distinguishes this film that is filled with many funny scenes. In addition to Fields' classic slapstick comedy, the final car chase scene is a near classic in this film genre. Abbott and Costello's *In Society* (1944), for example, repeated this scene. The selected scene is one of many observations Fields made in his films about human behavior and management.[21]

SCENES

DVD CHAPTER 3 NO RESPECT (0:04:11–0:06:31)

These scenes start with a fade-in shot of the front of a restaurant and The Great Man enters. This sequence appears early in the film following his sidewalk interactions with different people. It ends with The Great Man muttering, "Flies get the best of everything. Go away. Go away. Go away. Go on." The film cuts to Sound Stage 6 and The Great Man's niece (Gloria Jean) singing.

WHAT TO WATCH FOR AND ASK YOURSELF

- Does the waitress (Jody Gilbert) show concern for her customers?
- Is The Great Man a cranky customer who does not deserve careful service?
- What would you do in this situation, assuming you took it seriously?

---

[21] Ronald J. Fields and Shaun O'L. Higgins, *Never Give a Sucker and Even Break: W. C. Fields on Business* (Paramus, NJ: Prentice Hall Press, 2000); Maltin 2014, 995–96.

CONCEPTS OR EXAMPLES

☐ Customer focus (or absence)   ☐ Customer satisfaction

☐ Customer needs or desires   ☐ Customer behavior

ANALYSIS

_____

_____

_____

_____

_____

_____

_____

_____

_____

_____

_____

PERSONAL REACTIONS

_____

_____

_____

_____

_____

_____

_____

_____

_____

_____

CHAPTER 4
Technology

Changes in **technology** such as computing power and telecommunications will continue to revolutionize what people and organizations do in the future. High-speed processors, larger memory capacity, and broadband Internet connections have made desktop PCs ever more powerful business tools. Laptops, palmtops, smartphones, and tablets easily connect to the Internet and with each other from almost anywhere. Staying connected continues to get easier. Social networking sites such as facebook, Twitter, and LinkedIn are widely used.[22]

A revolution in materials technology is unfolding. Some materials already in use are carbon fiber composites and optical fibers, the basis of tennis rackets and communication cable respectively. Others, such as super polymers, amorphous metal alloys, and molecular transistors, add to a growing list of human created materials. Innovations in product ideas and technological solutions no longer depend on naturally existing materials.[23]

This chapter discusses the following films that show different technologies and their effects on behavior and organizations:

- *The Net*
- *The Saint*
- *My Best Friend's Wedding*
- *You've Got Mail*

Early scenes from *The Net* show the effects of the Internet on people's behavior. *The Saint* has scenes centered on fusion technology that shows its effects on power relationships. *My Best Friend's Wedding* has a closing sequence that shows technology-induced social interaction. *You've Got Mail* is about an interpersonal relationship that occurs over the Internet and in face-to-face interaction.

---

[22] Frances Cairncross, *The Death of Distance: How the Communication Revolution will Change Our Lives* (Boston: Harvard Business School Press 1997); Jesse Hempel, "How Facebook Is Taking Over Our Lives," *Fortune* (March 2, 2009): 48–56.

[23] Joseph E. Champoux, *Organizational Behavior: Integrating Individuals, Groups, and Organizations*, 4th ed. (New York: Taylor & Francis, 2011), 35–36; Neil Gross and Otis Port, "The Next WAVE," *Business Week* (August 24, 1998): 80, 82–83.

The Net

Color, 1995
Running Time: 1 hour, 54 minutes
Rating: PG-13
Director: Irwin Winkler
Distributor: Columbia TriStar Home Entertainment

Mousy computer systems analyst Angela Bennett (Sandra Bullock) discovers an Internet program that easily accesses classified databases. Others know what she has discovered and set out to eliminate her identity from various official records. Then they try to kill her.

SCENES

DVD CHAPTER 2 ANGELA BENNETT (0:03:33–0:08:07)

This sequence begins with shots of Angela assessing a video game for viruses. It ends after Angela says, "Yeah, I know." She turns off her computer. The film cuts to her mother (Diane Baker) playing the piano at an assisted living facility. Angela arrives for a visit.

WHAT TO WATCH FOR AND ASK YOURSELF

- Which technologies do these scenes show?
- What technological effects on social interaction do these scenes show?
- Is this an example of modern telecommuting–working from home or as part of a virtual team?

CONCEPTS OR EXAMPLES

- [ ] Various technologies
- [ ] Effects of technology on social interaction
- [ ] Telecommuting
- [ ] Virtual team
- [ ] Behavioral effects of technology

ANALYSIS

_____

_____

_____

_____

_____

_____

_____

_____

_____

PERSONAL REACTIONS

_____

_____

_____

_____

_____

_____

_____

_____

_____

The Saint

Color, 1997
Running Time: 1 hour, 58 minutes
Rating: PG-13
Director: Phillip Noyce
Distributor: Paramount Home Video

Russian strong man Ivan Tretiak (Rade Serbedzija) hires super thief and master of disguises Simon Templar (Val Kilmer) to steal a fusion formula from a beautiful scientist. Templar falls in love with Dr. Emma Russell (Eilsabeth Shue). He double-crosses Tretiak, setting in motion a series of action scenes in which Templar and Russell escape from danger. The film has many wonderful location shots of Oxford University and Moscow. True Saint fans might find this version closer to *Mission Impossible* than to earlier television and cinema versions of this appealing character from novelist Leslie Charteris.[24]

SCENES

DVD CHAPTER 19. REVELATION IN RED SQUARE TO CHAPTER 20. I KNOW YOU (1:38:13–1:42:15)

These scenes start as Ilya Tretiak (Valeri Nikolayev) puts a microphone on his father Ivan Tretiak. They follow President Karpov's (Evgeny Lazarev) arrest in his quarters. The scenes end after the fusion experiment works and the arrest of the Tretiaks. The film fades to an aerial shot of Scotland Yard. Chief Inspector Teal's (Alun Armstrong) voice-over says, "And he made no threat to contact you in the future"? Teal and Inspector Rabineau (Charlotte Cornwell) interview Dr. Russell about her association with The Saint.

WHAT TO WATCH FOR AND ASK YOURSELF

- Does Ivan Tretiak believe he has the power to overthrow President Karpov?
- Does the fusion technology change people's perception of Tretiak and Karpov's power?
- Can technology have such effects in real organizations?

---

24 Fox, Grant, and Imeson, *Seventh Virgin Film Guide*, 596.

CONCEPTS OR EXAMPLES

☐ Technology   ☐ Power relationships

☐ Power   ☐ Perceptions of power

☐ Power loss   ☐ Power gain

ANALYSIS

_____

_____

_____

_____

_____

_____

_____

_____

_____

_____

PERSONAL REACTIONS

_____

_____

_____

_____

_____

_____

_____

_____

_____

_____

My Best Friend's Wedding (I)

Color, 1997
Running Time: 1 hour, 45 minutes
Rating: PG-13
Director: P. J. Hogan
Distributor: Columbia TriStar Home Video

Sportswriter Michael O'Neal (Dermot Mulroney) and restaurant critic Julianne Potter (Julia Roberts) are best friends. They have agreed to marry each other if neither has found a partner by age 28. Michael falls for the wealthy and beautiful Kimmy (Cameron Diaz). Julianne now realizes she loves Michael and tries to stop the wedding. Her bungled efforts add great humor to the film. Beautifully photographed on location in Chicago.[25]

Note: Chapter 20 "Decision Making" also discusses scenes from this film.

SCENES

DVD CHAPTER 27 "THE WAY YOU LOOK TONIGHT" THROUGH CHAPTER 28 GEORGE CALLS (1:37:09–1:40:42)

These scenes start at the end of the film during Michael and Kimmy's wedding reception. The scenes open with a close-up of Julianne watching them leave. It ends with George (Rupert Everett) and Julianne dancing. The screen goes black and the film cuts to the closing credits.

WHAT TO WATCH FOR AND ASK YOURSELF

- Does technology affect social interaction in these scenes? How?
- Could technology have similar effects in real organizations?
- George is a homosexual; Julianne is a heterosexual. Do these differences keep them apart?

---

[25] Craddock, *VideoHound's Golden Movie Retriever*, 712.

CONCEPTS OR EXAMPLES

☐ Technology   ☐ Attraction as lovers

☐ Social interaction   ☐ Cellular telephones

                              ☐ Attraction as friends

ANALYSIS

_____

_____

_____

_____

_____

_____

_____

_____

_____

_____

PERSONAL REACTIONS

_____

_____

_____

_____

_____

_____

_____

_____

_____

Joseph E. Champoux

You've Got Mail

Color, 1998
Running Time: 2 hours
Rating: PG
Director: Nora Ephron
Distributor: Warner Home Video

Neighborhood bookstore owner Kathleen Kelly (Meg Ryan) regularly interacts over the Internet with superstore head Joe Fox (Tom Hanks). The anonymity of Internet interactions disguises their identities. Kathleen eventually meets Joe Fox, but does not know he is the same person in her Internet interactions. Joe also does not know that Kathleen is his Internet partner. A charming, warm remake of the 1940 film *The Shop Around the Corner* in which the technology for interaction is the U.S. mail.[26]

SCENES

Two sets of scenes offer strong contrasts in social interaction. The first set shows Internet interaction. The second shows face-to-face interaction. Try to predict their face-to-face interaction before watching the second set of scenes.

DVD CHAPTER 2 MORNING LOG-ONS. TO CHAPTER 4 CYBERROMANTICS. (0:03:34–0:08:39)

These scenes appear early in the film after the opening credits. Frank Navasky (Greg Kinnear) and Kathleen begin their day. He leaves for work. Kathleen comes out of the bathroom and logs on to America Online. These scenes end as Joe Fox approaches a shrouded building—the site of his new superstore. The film cuts to the store's interior with Joe discussing construction status with Kevin Jackson (Dave Chappelle).

DVD CHAPTER 10 WHO'S WORRIED? THROUGH CHAPTER 11 PARTY PATTER. (0:32:35–0:38:24)

These scenes follow discussions about the effect of the Fox superstore on the sales of Kathleen's shop. They start with Frank's voice-over saying, "A nut? She called me a nut?" Frank and Kathleen walk to a party in the evening while having a conversation. The scenes end as the two couples separate and Joe says to Patricia Eden (Parker Posey), "Hey hon, have you ever had a caviar garnish?" The film cuts to Joe and Patricia preparing for bed. Patricia talks about Frank.

WHAT TO WATCH FOR AND ASK YOURSELF

- What effect does anonymity have on Kathleen and Joe's Internet interactions?
- Do you expect their face-to-face interaction to differ? Why and how?
- Can anonymous Internet interactions have similar effects in organizations?

---

[26] Ibid., 1145.

CONCEPTS OR EXAMPLES

☐ Verbal communication   ☐ Anonymity

☐ Internet interaction   ☐ Face-to-face interaction

☐ Nonverbal communication   ☐ Lack of anonymity

☐ Behavioral reactions

ANALYSIS

_____

_____

_____

_____

_____

_____

_____

_____

_____

_____

PERSONAL REACTIONS

_____

_____

_____

_____

_____

_____

_____

_____

_____

CHAPTER 5
International Context

The **global environment** of organizations demands an international focus of modern managers. Now, the world is their environment and will become increasingly so in the future. For some organizations, thinking internationally means finding new markets outside the home country; for others, becoming a multinational organization operating in many countries; and for others becoming a transnational organization whose decisions are not limited by country boundaries. Modern managers must think of the entire planet as a source of labor and materials, places of production, and markets.[27]

Regional trade agreements are opening vast new markets, possibly increasing a firm's competition.[28] The North American Free Trade Agreement (NAFTA) of 1994 opened the borders of Mexico, Canada, and the United States to easy movement of goods, capital, and services.[29] Europe took similar steps to encourage freer trade among its countries. The movement of 12 European countries to a single currency, the euro (€), should enhance free trade among its users.[30]

[27] William B. Johnston, "Global Workforce 2000: The New World Labor Market," *Harvard Business Review* 69, no. 2 (1991): 115–129; R. I. Kirkland, Jr., "Entering a New Age of Boundless Competition," *Fortune* (March 14, 1988): 40–48.

[28] C. Michael Aho and Sylvia Ostry, "Regional Trading Blocs: Pragmatic or Problematic Policy?" in *The Global Economy: America's Role in the Decade Ahead*, ed. William Emerson Brock and Robert D. Hormats (New York: W. W. Norton, 1990): 147–173; Sylvia Ostry, "Governments and Corporations in a Shrinking World: Trade and Innovation Policies in the United States, Europe, and Japan," *Columbia Journal of World Business* 25, no. 1/2 (1990): 10–16.

[29] B. Davis and J. Calmes, "The House Passes Nafta–Trade Win: House Approves Nafta, Providing President With Crucial Victory," *The Wall Street Journal* (November 18, 1993): A1.

[30] David Fairlamb, "Ready, Set, Euros!" *Business Week* (July 2, 2001): 48–50; Justin Fox, "Europe Is Heading for a Wild Ride," *Fortune* (August 17, 1998): 145–46, 148–49.

Cinema is a powerful source of cross-cultural experiences.[31] Scenes from the following films will introduce you to the international context of organizations:

- *French Kiss*
- *Tampopo (Dandelion)*
- *Mississippi Masala*
- *Ciao, Professore!*

French Kiss shows a stereotypical view of the French. *Tampopo (Dandelion)*, a Japanese film, has a satirical view of Japanese eating styles, conformity, and deviant behavior. *Mississippi Masala* offers a view of East Indian culture. *Ciao, Professore!*, an Italian film, offers some observations on Italian culture.

---

[31] Joseph E. Champoux, "European Films as a Management Education Teaching Resource," In T. Torres Coronas, M. Gascó Hernández, and A. Fernandes de Matos Coelho (eds.), *Changing the Way You Teach: Creative Tools for Management Educators* (Oviedo, Spain: Septem Ediciones, 2005), 85–106.

French Kiss

Color, 1995
Running Time: 1 hour, 51 minutes
Rating: PG-13
Director: Lawrence Kasdan
Distributor: Twentieth Century Fox Home Entertainment

Jilted Kate (Meg Ryan) goes to Paris to pursue her fiancée Charlie (Timothy Hutton). Although scared of flying, Kate gets the support of her seat partner Luc Teyssier (Kevin Kline), a French thief. Kate's stereotype of French men rules her behavior, but she and Luc eventually develop a close relationship. This is a light, charming film with many wonderful scenes of France.

SCENES

DVD CHAPTER 7. AFTER THE BAGS (0:30:31–0:35:10)

These scenes follow Kate's extended interactions in the lobby of the Hotel George V after her arrival in Paris. They start as Kate and Luc quickly leave the hotel and Kate calls the concierge (Laurent Spielvogel) a "bastard". Luc says, "All right, all right. Uh, you wait here. I'll go get the…my car and we go get your stuff. O.K.?" The scenes end after Kate and Luc walk past the Metropolitain (subway) station entrance. After some discussion Luc concludes, "I'm back in business, OK?" The film cuts to Bob (François Cluzet) in his apartment.

WHAT TO WATCH FOR AND ASK YOURSELF

- Which parts of these scenes give you the most contrast with your home culture?
- Do you feel these scenes accurately show at least some Frenchmen's behavior? Why or why not?
- Are there any implications of these scenes for a foreigner entering a new culture?

CONCEPTS OR EXAMPLES

☐ Cultural differences   ☐ Entering another culture

☐ Stereotypes   ☐ Architectural differences

☐ First impressions

ANALYSIS

_____

_____

_____

_____

_____

_____

_____

_____

_____

_____

PERSONAL REACTIONS

_____

_____

_____

_____

_____

_____

_____

_____

_____

_____

_____

Tampopo (Dandelion)

Color, 1985
Japanese with English subtitles
Running Time: 1 hour, 54 minutes
Rating: NR
Director: Juzo Itami
Distributor: Fox Lorber Home Video[32]

This comedy satire offers an irreverent look at several aspects of Japanese society, especially the role of food and eating styles. Truck driver Goro (Tsutomu Yamazaki) tries to help Tampopo (Nobuko Miyamoto) develop a successful noodle shop. This film was highly popular in Japan, suggesting it showed Japanese society's reality from a fresh viewpoint. The late director Juzo Itami, emerged in the 1980s as an irreverent cinematic observer of Japanese society.[33] *Warning*: Viewing this film will greatly increase your desire for noodles.

SCENES

DVD CHAPTER 5 TO CHAPTER 6 (0:19:25–0:26:46)

This sequence starts with a shot of a tall building which houses the restaurant in which a group of business men will dine. It follows the shots of Tampopo cooling down after jogging while Goro sits on his bicycle blowing a whistle. Several businessmen enter a private room in the restaurant. The sequence ends as the camera pans away from the women eating noodles.

WHAT TO WATCH FOR AND ASK YOURSELF

- Which aspects of Japanese culture do you immediately notice in this sequence?
- What is your reaction to the businessmen's behavior in the restaurant?
- How would you feel if you were in a restaurant in Japan and observed people eating noodles as these scenes show?

---

[32] Also available from "umbrella word cinema DVD" 2010. The chapters and scene position information are the same as shown above.

[33] Fox, Grant, and Imeson, *Seventh Virgin Film Guide*, 692.

CONCEPTS OR EXAMPLES

☐ Cross-cultural behavior
☐ Stereotypes
☐ Cultural norms

☐ Cross-cultural diversity
☐ Reactions in different cultures

ANALYSIS

_____

_____

_____

_____

_____

_____

_____

_____

_____

_____

PERSONAL REACTIONS

_____

_____

_____

_____

_____

_____

_____

_____

_____

_____

Mississippi Masala

Color, 1992
Running Time: 1 hour, 58 minutes
Rating: R
Director: Mira Nair
Distributor: The Samuel Goldwyn Company

A warm, engaging story about interracial romance between an African-American man and an East Indian woman. The film traces the effects on Indian families after their ouster from Idi Amin's Uganda and their move to Greenwood, Mississippi. "Masala" is a mix of spices and perhaps a reference to this film's wonderfully developed and colorful characters.[34]

SCENES

DVD CHAPTER 6. A TRADITIONAL INDIAN WEDDING (0:27:32–0:30:15)

These scenes start with a shot of a lighted motel sign, "Motel Monte Cristo." Some letters are not lit. They follow Demetrius' (Denzel Washington) discussion with his father in Lusco's restaurant. The sequence ends as Mina (Sarita Choudhury) and Harry Patel (Ashok Lath) leave the wedding reception. The film cuts to the motel reception desk.

WHAT TO WATCH FOR AND ASK YOURSELF

- Which aspects of East Indian culture capture your attention while viewing these scenes?
- Do they show any values that are important in Indian culture?
- Do you now understand some limited aspects of East Indian culture from viewing these scenes? What are they?

---

[34] Craddock, *VideoHound's Golden Movie Retriever*, 688.

CONCEPTS OR EXAMPLES

- ☐ Cross-cultural experience
- ☐ Physical characteristics of culture
- ☐ Cultural values
- ☐ Stereotypes
- ☐ Understanding other cultures
- ☐ Cross-cultural diversity

ANALYSIS

_____

_____

_____

_____

_____

_____

_____

_____

_____

_____

PERSONAL REACTIONS

_____

_____

_____

_____

_____

_____

_____

_____

_____

_____

Ciao, Professore!

Color, 1992
Italian with English Subtitles
Running Time: 1 hour, 31 minutes
Rating: R
Director: Lina Wertmüller
Distributor: Miramax Home Entertainment

Lina Wertmüller's charming film shows the relationships that develop between a school teacher and his elementary school students. An administrative error mistakenly transfers Marco Tulio Sperelli (Paolo Villaggio) to a run-down school in Southern Italy. Set in Corzano, a small town near Naples, he tries to change the lives of his students and undergoes change himself. Great wit and charm come from the amateur child actors who play Sperelli's students.[35]

SCENES

DVD CHAPTER 1 OPENING CREDITS: CORZANO! (0:00:01–0:07:22)

This sequence begins the film after a dark screen. It starts with a shot of a ship in a bay and the opening credits. Sperelli drives his Volkswagen Beetle along the bay while listening to Louis Armstrong. The sequence ends after Sperelli exclaims, "Corzano!"

WHAT TO WATCH FOR AND ASK YOURSELF

- What aspects of Italian culture appear in these scenes?
- Is Italian culture the same throughout the country?
- Using the experience of these scenes, would you like to visit Italy? Why or why not?

---

[35] Ibid., 224.

CONCEPTS OR EXAMPLES

☐ Culture   ☐ Stories and parables

☐ Physical characteristics of culture   ☐ Cultural differences

☐ Foreign language   ☐ Cultural values

ANALYSIS

_____

_____

_____

_____

_____

_____

_____

_____

_____

PERSONAL REACTIONS

_____

_____

_____

_____

_____

_____

_____

_____

_____

CHAPTER 6
Ethics and Behavior in Organizations

Ethical behavior is behavior viewed as right and honorable. **Unethical behavior** is behavior viewed as wrong and dishonorable. These straightforward definitions raise tough questions for managers and their organizations. First, what standards should they use to judge behavior as ethical or unethical? Second, how should one define the adjectives used to distinguish ethical from unethical behavior? *Right* and *wrong* have different meanings to different people. Standards of ethical behavior also vary from one country to another.[36]

Social responsibility of organizations emphasizes the effects of management decisions on the organization's external environment. It asks managers to consider the social and environmental effects of decisions, not only economic effects.[37]

Questions of ethics and social responsibility abound in organizations and affect management decisions. Is it ethical for an organization to withhold product safety information? Is it ethical for a person to use knowledge of human perception to affect the perception of an organization's customers or employees? Is it ethical for an organization to refuse to continuously improve the quality of its products or services when customers do not demand it? Those are only three ethical questions from an almost endless list that managers face.

The following films show ethics and behavior in organizations:

- *Grumpier Old Men*
- *The Godfather*
- *Other People's Money*
- *Scent of a Woman*

The lighter side of ethics and ethical dilemmas appears in scenes from *Grumpier Old Men*. Scenes from *The Godfather* offer dramatic and violent observations on ethical dilemmas. *Other People's Money* has scenes showing two people trying to persuade shareholders to accept their proposals—an example of ethics in the context of persuasive communication. The scenes from *Scent of a Woman* are outstanding demonstrations of the meaning of ethical behavior.

---

[36] Richard B. Brandt, *Ethical Theory: The Problems of Normative and Critical Ethics*, (Englewood Cliffs, NJ: Prentice Hall, 1959); Rogene A. Buchholz, *Fundamental Concepts and Problems in Business Ethics*, (Englewood Cliffs, NJ: Prentice Hall, 1989), chap. 1; Ronald N. Green and Aine Donovan, "The Methods of Business Ethics," in *The Oxford Handbook of Business Ethics*, eds. George G. Brenkert and Tom L. Beauchamp (New York: Oxford University Press, Inc., 2009), chap. 1.

[37] Donna J. Wood, "Corporate Social Performance Revisited," *Academy of Management Review* 16, no. 4 (1991): 691–718.

Grumpier Old Men

Color, 1995
Running Time: 1 hour, 41 minutes
Rating: PG-13
Director: Howard Deutch
Distributor: Warner Home Video

This sequel to *Grumpy Old Men* (1993) features the same two grumps: Max Goldman (Walter Matthau) and John Gustafson (Jack Lemmon). It is a light-hearted comedy showing the lifelong relationship of two next-door neighbors. They constantly argue and insult each other but are actually good friends, especially when fishing. Their lifelong goal: catch the biggest, most elusive catfish in the lake, Catfish Hunter.

SCENES

DVD CHAPTER 26 SOMETHING FISHY. TO CHAPTER 27 WHERE HE BELONGS. (1:23:39–1:30:15)

These scenes start with Max and John approaching John's car to go to Max's wedding. The scenes follow Max's marriage proposal to Maria (Sophia Loren). They end on the lake as Max realizes he and John are late for the wedding. Max races the boat to shore and they drive to the church. Max sings "Get me to the church on time."

WHAT TO WATCH FOR AND ASK YOURSELF

- Do Max and John behave ethically or unethically?
- Do they face ethical dilemmas? How many?
- What ethical theories (guidelines) do they use to decide a course of action?

CONCEPTS OR EXAMPLES

- ☐ Ethical behavior
- ☐ Ethical dilemmas
- ☐ Utilitarianism
- ☐ Rights theory

- ☐ Justice theory
- ☐ Egoism
- ☐ Unethical behavior

ANALYSIS

_____

_____

_____

_____

_____

_____

_____

_____

PERSONAL REACTIONS

_____

_____

_____

_____

_____

_____

_____

_____

_____

_____

The Godfather (I)

Color, 1972
Running Time: 2 hours, 51 minutes
Rating: R
Director: Francis Ford Coppola
Distributor: Paramount Home Video

This film, based on Mario Puzo's novel, is a powerful look at a Mafia family led by Don Corleone (Marlon Brando). It is an intense film that roams through the personal lives of its characters and shows the fiercely violent side of organized crime. The film suggests stunning parallels between managing a gangster organization and managing an organization of any other type. An irresistible work, *The Godfather* is filled with memorable scenes and memorable performances. The American Film Institute in 1998 ranked this film in the top 100 American films.[38]

Note: Chapter 10, "Organizational Culture" and Chapter 21 "Power and Political Behavior" discuss other scenes from this film.

SCENES

DVD CHAPTER 21. BAPTISM AND MURDER (2:36:18–2:41:18)

This sequence starts after Don Corleone's funeral. It opens with a shot inside the church where the baptism of Connie's (Talia Shire) baby (Sofia Coppola) begins. Organ music plays in the background. The sequence ends after the priest says, "Michael Rizzi, go in peace. And may the Lord be with you. Amen." The film cuts to outside the church with bells ringing. The baby in this baptismal scene is director Francis Ford Coppola's infant daughter Sofia.[39] These scenes have several R-rated violent moments.

WHAT TO WATCH FOR AND ASK YOURSELF

- What ethical dilemma does Michael face in these scenes?
- How does he manage his way through the dilemma?
- Are such dilemmas a believable part of modern life? Try to recall some examples from your experience.

---

[38] Craddock, *VideoHound's Golden Movie Retriever*, 429.
[39] Ibid.

CONCEPTS OR EXAMPLES

- ☐ Ethical behavior
- ☐ Unethical behavior
- ☐ Legal behavior

- ☐ Ethical dilemma
- ☐ Illegal behavior

ANALYSIS

_____

_____

_____

_____

_____

_____

_____

_____

_____

_____

_____

PERSONAL REACTIONS

_____

_____

_____

_____

_____

_____

_____

_____

_____

_____

Other People's Money

Color, 1991
Running Time: 1 hour, 51 minutes
Rating: R
Director: Norman Jewison
Distributor: Warner Home Video

Lawrence Garfield (Danny DeVito) is a strong-willed Wall Street investment banker. His reputation of buying and liquidating companies precedes him as he sets out to acquire New England Wire & Cable Company. The 86-year-old company in a small Rhode Island town is the townspeople's main source of employment. Although other divisions of the company are profitable, the wire and cable division is losing money. Chairman of the Board Andrew Jorgenson (Gregory Peck) has deep personal ties to the company his father founded. He also has a deep commitment to his employees and tries to fight Garfield's takeover effort.

See Graham, Peña, and Kocher (1999) for a corporate restructuring and finance application of this film. They discuss several scenes with ethical implications in these areas.[40]

SCENES

DVD CHAPTER 20 FUNERAL WORTH HAVING. (1:24:41–1:30:39)

These scenes begin with company president Bill Coles (Dean Jones) approaching the microphone. He introduces Garfield following Jorgenson's presentation of his arguments. These scenes end after Garfield presents his case. The film continues with the shareholders' vote.

WHAT TO WATCH FOR AND ASK YOURSELF

- Which ethical theory (guideline) dominates Garfield's arguments?
- Does he express concern for employees and the community?
- What does he emphasize for shareholders to consider in their decision?

---

[40] Lise Graham, Leticia Peña, and Claudia Kocher, "*Other People's Money*: A Visual Technology for Teaching Corporate Restructuring Cross-functionally," *Journal of Management Education* 23, no. 1 (1999): 53–64.

Joseph E. Champoux

CONCEPTS OR EXAMPLES

- [ ] Ethical behavior
- [ ] Utilitarianism
- [ ] Rights theory
- [ ] Justice theory
- [ ] Unethical behavior
- [ ] Ethical decision making
- [ ] Social responsibility

ANALYSIS

_____

_____

_____

_____

_____

_____

_____

_____

_____

PERSONAL REACTIONS

_____

_____

_____

_____

_____

_____

_____

_____

_____

_____

Scent of a Woman

Color, 1992
Running Time: 2 hours, 37 minutes
Rating: R
Director: Martin Brest
Distributor: Universal Home Video

Young Charlie Simms (Chris O'Donnell) wants to earn extra money over Thanksgiving weekend for air fare to go home during his Christmas break. He becomes a guide and caretaker for blind, ill-tempered, retired, Lt. Colonel Frank Slade (Al Pacino). Charlie, from Gresham, Oregon, is quiet and reserved and has had little experience with the opposite sex. He attends the exclusive Baird Preparatory School on a scholarship. His wild New York City weekend with Frank Slade bonds them forever. This film is a remake of *Profumo di Donna*, a 1975 Italian film.[41]

Charlie and another student, George Willis, Jr. (Philip Seymour Hoffman), had seen three students vandalize the headmaster's new Jaguar. Under repeated questioning by the headmaster, neither Charlie nor George identify the students. The headmaster pressures Charlie by noting that his career depends on the headmaster's support for him to go to Harvard University.

SCENES

DVD CHAPTER 12 AN OPENING MEETING TO CHAPTER 13 THE COLONEL SPEAKS OUT (2:11:52–2:26:06)

These scenes start with Mr. Trask (James Rebhorn), the headmaster, walking down the aisle of the school's chapel. The scenes are the joint faculty-student hearing called by Mr. Trask to settle the vandalism incident and decide Charlie's and George's fate. These scenes are at the end of the film after Charlie and Lt. Colonel Slade return from their New York City weekend. They end after Slade's supportive speech. This sequence has some R-rated language.

WHAT TO WATCH FOR AND ASK YOURSELF

- Does George Willis, Jr. behave ethically or unethically?
- Does Charlie Simms behave ethically or unethically?
- Do other people (Mr. Trask, George Willis, Sr. (Baxter Harris), committee members) in these scenes behave ethically or unethically?

---

[41] Craddock, *VideoHound's Golden Movie Retriever*, 887.

CONCEPTS OR EXAMPLES

- ☐ Ethical behavior
- ☐ Unethical behavior

- ☐ Utilitarianism
- ☐ Ethical dilemma

- ☐ Justice theory
- ☐ Difficulty in behaving according to personal values
- ☐ Freely chosen behavior
- ☐ Rights theory

ANALYSIS

_____

_____

_____

_____

_____

_____

_____

_____

_____

_____

PERSONAL REACTIONS

_____

_____

_____

_____

_____

_____

_____

_____

_____

CHAPTER 7
Perception

Perception is a cognitive process that lets a person make sense of stimuli from the environment. These stimuli affect all senses: sight, touch, taste, smell, and hearing. They can come from other people, events, physical objects, or ideas. The **perceptual process** includes both the inputs to the person and the selection of inputs to which the person attends. A person's perceptual process learns from repeated exposure to stimuli and stores recallable images that process inputs faster later. The perceptual process helps a person adapt to a changing environment.[42]

A **target** is the object of a person's perceptual process, such as another person, a physical object, an event, a sound, an idea, or a concept. **Threshold** is the minimum amount of information from a target for a person to notice its presence. The **detection threshold** is the point at which a person notices that something has changed in the environment. The **recognition threshold** is the point at which a person can identify the target or changes in the target.

Perceptual errors include perceptual set and stereotyping. **Perceptual set** are beliefs based on previous experience with the target. These beliefs act like a set of instructions that process information the person gets about the target.[43] A **stereotype** is a perceptual set that holds beliefs and perceived attributes of a target person based on the group to which the person belongs.

Scenes from four films show some key perception issues:

- *The Little Mermaid*
- *Two Much*
- *Antz*
- *Twice Upon a Yesterday*

The Little Mermaid presents a stereotype of a French chef. *Two Much* shows how social perception varies. *Antz* has a captivating set of animated scenes that show how the nature of a perceptual target affects one's perception of it. *Twice Upon a Yesterday*, a British film, also shows social perception in two parallel scenes.

---

[42] Soledad Ballesteros, "Cognitive Approaches to Human Perception: Introduction," in *Cognitive Approaches to Human Perception*, ed. Soledad Ballesteros (Hillsdale, NJ: Lawrence Erlbaum Associates, 1994), chap. 1; William N. Dember, *Psychology of Perception* (New York: Holt, Rinehart and Winston, 1960); Robert L. Goldstone, "Perceptual Learning," in *Annual Review of Psychology*, vol. 49, ed. Janet T. Spence, John M. Darley, and Donald J. Foss (Palo Alto: Annual Reviews, Inc., 1998), 585–612.

[43] Jules B. Davidoff, *Differences in Visual Perception: The Individual Eye* (London: Crosby Lockwood Stapes, 1975), 167–77.

The Little Mermaid

Color, 1989
Running Time: 1 hour, 23 minutes
Rating: G
Director: John Musker, Ron Clements
Distributor: Walt Disney Studios Home Entertainment

Disney's adaptation of the famous Hans Christian Andersen fable will enchant any viewer. Ariel (voiced by Jodi Benson), a teenage mermaid, falls in love with handsome surface dweller Prince Eric (voiced by Chris Barnes) after saving him from a shipwreck. Ariel's father King Triton (voiced by Kenneth Mars) has forbidden her and all other sea creatures to have contact with the surface. Ariel negotiates with Ursula, the evil sea witch (voiced by Pat Carroll), to become human so she can pursue Prince Eric. She trades her voice for legs and pursues the prince. Adventure, romance, and great Broadway-style songs complete the rest of the film.[44]

SCENES

DVD CHAPTER 19 "LES POISSONS" (0:52:02–0:55:08)

This sequence starts shortly after Ariel's arrival at Eric's castle. Sebastian the Crab (voiced by Samuel E. Wright) has entered the castle's kitchen. He sees seafood in preparation and becomes alarmed. The film cuts briefly to the dining room, where Ariel enters in her new clothes. It returns to Sebastian's adventure at the hands of Chef Louis (voiced by René Auberjonois). This sequence ends as Grimsby (Ben Wright) looks at his empty plate with surprise. The scenes dissolve to Ariel looking into the night from her bedroom window.

WHAT TO WATCH FOR AND ASK YOURSELF

- What is your impression of Chef Louis?
- To what do you attribute his behavior?
- Is this an accurate portrayal of a French chef or a caricature based on stereotype?

---

[44] Champoux, "Animated Films," 78–99.

CONCEPTS OR EXAMPLES

- ☐ Perceptual set
- ☐ Perceptual errors
- ☐ Stereotype
- ☐ Target
- ☐ Attribution process

ANALYSIS

_____

_____

_____

_____

_____

_____

_____

_____

_____

_____

PERSONAL REACTIONS

_____

_____

_____

_____

_____

_____

_____

_____

_____

Two Much

Color, 1996
Running Time: 1 hour, 58 minutes
Rating: PG-13
Director: Fernando Trueba
Distributor: Buena Vista Home Entertainment

Art Dodge (Antonio Banderas) wants to break off his engagement to Betty Kerner (Melanie Griffith). Her mob boss ex-husband pressures him to go through with the wedding. Art meets Betty's sister Liz (Daryl Hannah) and falls in love with her. Art creates his twin brother Bart (Antonio Banderas) so he can pursue Liz. Predictable results occur along the way, but with many funny scenes.

SCENES

There are two sets of scenes. Set 1 shows Liz Kerner's first meeting with Art Dodge. Set 2 shows her first meeting with Bart Dodge.[45]

DVD CHAPTER 3. THE MISUNDERSTANDING (0:17:27–0:20:21)

The first scenes start as Art opens the shower door and meets Liz whom he thinks is Betty. These scenes follow his engagement to Betty. The scenes end after Liz says goodbye and walks away. Betty and Art continue talking. The film cuts to a shot of a newspaper showing Betty's planned marriage to Art.

DVD CHAPTER 6. COURTING LIZ (0:45:29–0:48:27)

The second scenes start as Bart enters Betty and Liz's home and Conchita (Theodora Castellanos) the housekeeper greets him. Liz meets Bart for the first time. These scenes follow Art's first meeting of Betty's ex-husband (twice) Gene (Danny Aiello). They end after Gene's yacht arrives. Liz says, "My ex-brother-in-law. He's big on drama." Bart says, "Unlike your sister."

WHAT TO WATCH FOR AND ASK YOURSELF

- What characteristics of Art and Bart affect Liz's perception of them?
- What aspects of social perception do these scenes show?
- Does Liz use stereotypes to characterize Art and Bart?

---

[45] A triple feature collection distributed by Mill Creek Entertainment includes *Two Much*. The Scene Selection menu only shows the chapter numbers. The start and stop positions are the same as shown above.

CONCEPTS OR EXAMPLES

☐ Perception   ☐ Perceptual errors

☐ Social perception   ☐ Perceptual process

☐ Stereotype   ☐ Target(s)

☐ Perceptual accuracy

ANALYSIS

_____

_____

_____

_____

_____

_____

_____

_____

_____

_____

PERSONAL REACTIONS

_____

_____

_____

_____

_____

_____

_____

_____

_____

_____

Antz (II)

Color, 1998
Running Time: 1 hour, 23 minutes
Rating: PG
Director: Eric Darnell, Tim Johnson
Distributor: DreamWorks Home Entertainment

Z (voiced by Woody Allen) is an insignificant worker ant in a massive ant colony. He is trying to find his role in life and pursue Princess Bala (voiced by Sharon Stone). Everything changes after he trades places with his soldier ant friend Weaver (voiced by Sylvester Stallone). A termite war and the pursuit of the evil General Mandible (voiced by Gene Hackman) take Z's life to new and unexpected places. It helps us imagine our world, organizations, and ourselves from the perspective of some wonderfully animated insect creatures.[46]

Note: Chapter 1 "Introduction to Organizations and Management" discusses other scenes from this film.

SCENES

DVD CHAPTER 16. THE PLASTIC-WRAPPED PARADISE THROUGH CHAPTER 17. TERROR FROM ABOVE (0:47:56–0:53:33)

These scenes start after Princess Bala awakens from resting following her first day with Z on their trip to find Insectopia. General Mandible had shortly before told the colony that Z kidnapped Bala. Princess Bala separates the grass and exclaims, "Ohh! Oh my God. Z! Come here!" The scenes end after the boy uses a penny to remove the gum from his shoe and throws the coin into a trash heap. The film cuts to General Mandible's soldier ants torturing Weaver.

WHAT TO WATCH FOR AND ASK YOURSELF

- The perceptual targets in these scenes are soda cans, sandwiches, a thermos bottle, and the like. Are these ambiguous or unambiguous targets to Z and Princess Bala?
- Are these high- or low-contrast targets?
- Does the target's size help them standout?

---

[46] From CHAMPOUX ICO. *Organizational Behavior*, 1e. © 2001 South-Western, a part of Cengage Learning, Inc. Reproduced by permission. www.cengage.com/permissions

62

CONCEPTS OR EXAMPLES

☐ Target(s)   ☐ Ambiguous target
☐ Perceptual process   ☐ High contrast target
☐ Detection threshold   ☐ Unambiguous target
☐ Target size   ☐ Recognition threshold

ANALYSIS

_____

_____

_____

_____

_____

_____

_____

_____

_____

PERSONAL REACTIONS

_____

_____

_____

_____

_____

_____

_____

_____

_____

_____

Twice Upon a Yesterday

Color, 1998
Running Time: 1 hour, 31 minutes
Rating: R
Director: Maria Ripoll
Distributor: Trimark Pictures

Victor Bukowski's (Douglas Henshall) six year and twenty-five day relationship with beautiful Sylvia Weld (Lena Headey) sours after he tells the truth about having an affair. An accidental meeting with two magical trash collectors lets him relive the day where he tries another approach—not saying anything about it to Sylvia. Along the way, he meets the captivating Louise (Penélope Cruz), an encounter that changes his attraction to Sylvia. The film comes to an unusual close, leaving the viewer wondering about Sylvia's next step.

SCENES

There are two scenes showing Victor's approaches to his dilemma with Sylvia. Each shows different aspects of social perception and different behavioral results.

DVD CHAPTER 4. CARNIVAL (0:10:54–0:13:50)

These scenes follow Victor's encounter with the Notting Hill Carnival. He enters the flat while saying, "Anyway... I finally arrived home." Sylvia questions his activities before arriving. The scenes end after Sylvia throws a guitar to the floor.

DVD CHAPTER 6. LET GO TO CHAPTER 7. GUILT (0:21:25–0:26:26)

This sequence starts with Victor twirling on the street. He falls and discovers he is in the middle of the Notting Hill Carnival. These scenes follow his "disenchantment" experience with trash collectors Rafael (Gustavo Salmerón) and Don Miguel (Eusebio Lázaro). The sequence ends with Victor and Sylvia falling onto the bed after he asks her to marry him. The film cuts to Victor coming out of the bed covers.

WHAT TO WATCH FOR AND ASK YOURSELF

- What is the basis of Sylvia's social perception of Victor in each instance?
- What information did she attend to when forming her impression of Victor?
- Which is the more correct behavior for Victor—telling the truth or not commenting at all?

CONCEPTS OR EXAMPLES

- ☐ Social perception
- ☐ Impression formation
- ☐ Observations of person
- ☐ Observations of situation

ANALYSIS

_____

_____

_____

_____

_____

_____

_____

_____

_____

_____

_____

PERSONAL REACTIONS

_____

_____

_____

_____

_____

_____

_____

_____

_____

_____

CHAPTER 8
Attitudes

Attitudes play a key role in social psychology because of the presumed connection between people's perceptions of their world and their behavior in it. Managers also consider attitudes important. They commonly attribute a person's poor work performance to a bad work attitude.

An **attitude** is "a learned predisposition to respond in a consistently favorable or unfavorable manner with respect to a given object".[47] An attitude object is anything in a person's environment, including physical objects, issues, ideas, events, and people. The evaluative or affective part of the definition is central to the concept. It distinguishes an attitude from other psychological concepts such as need, motive, and trait.[48]

Attitudes are dynamic and change over time. The sources of change are within the person and in the person's social environment. **Attitude change** happens because (1) something persuades the person to shift his or her attitude, (2) the norms of a social group important to the person affect his or her attitude, or (3) the person becomes uncomfortable with some aspects of his or her beliefs about certain matters.[49]

Several scenes from the following films show the meaning of attitudes, their behavioral connections, and how attitudes form and change:

- *Joe Versus the Volcano*
- *Clockwatchers*
- *Office Space*
- *The Guilt Trip*

The opening scenes of *Joe Versus the Volcano* comically show some negative work attitudes. The *Clockwatchers* scenes show satirically and symbolically the attitudes and behavior of a group of temporary workers. *Office Space* has some opening scenes that have behavioral evidence of the work attitudes of a computer programmer and his coworkers. The scenes from *The Guilt Trip* show the varying attitudes of a mother and her son preparing for an eight day road trip.

---

[47] Martin Fishbein and Icek Ajzen. *Belief, Attitude, Intention and Behavior: An Introduction to Theory and Research* (Reading, MA: Addison-Wesley, 1975), 6.

[48] Ibid., 6–11; Timothy A. Judge and John D. Kammeyer-Mueller, "Job Attitudes," *Annual Review of Psychology* 63, (2012): 341–67; Gregory R. Maio and Geoffrey Haddock, *The Psychology of Attitudes and Attitude Change* (London: Sage Publications, Ltd., 2009).

[49] William J. McGuire, "Attitudes and Attitude Change," in *Handbook of Social Psychology*, vol. I, ed. Gardner Lindzey and Elliot Aronson (New York: Random House, 1985), 233–346.

Joe Versus the Volcano (I)

Color, 1990
Running Time: 1 hour, 42 minutes
Rating: PG
Director: John Patrick Shanley
Distributor: *Warner Home Video*

"Once upon a time there was a guy named Joe who had a very lousy job..." This film's opening title screens give strong clues about a typical workday for Joe Banks (Tom Hanks). He has a bad job and perhaps an even worse work environment. Joe does not feel well. He learns from his doctor that he has a "brain cloud," a rare disease that will kill him in less than six months. He accepts millionaire Samuel Harvey Graynamore's (Lloyd Bridges) offer of a vacation on Waponi Woo, a South Sea Island where he will live like a king. The bad part of the vacation comes when he learns he must jump into a local volcano as part of an island ritual.

Note: Chapter 14 "Intrinsic Rewards and Job Design" also discusses scenes from this film.

SCENES

DVD CHAPTER 1 GRINDING/CREDITS. (0:00:33–0:05:07)

These scenes begin the film. They start with the title screen, "Once upon a time there was a guy named Joe." The scenes end after Joe Banks punches his timecard and goes into his office. The early part of these scenes brims with cinematic reference to Fritz Lang's *Metropolis* (1927), his expressionist allegory about the oppressed working class.[50]

WHAT TO WATCH FOR AND ASK YOURSELF

- What types of work attitudes do the workers have—positive or negative? What are the attitude objects?
- Can you see a link between the attitudes of these workers and their behavior?
- Have you ever experienced a similar situation?

---

[50] Kenneth Jurkiewicz, "Using Film in the Humanities Classroom: The Case of *Metropolis*," *English Journal* 79, no. 3 (1990): 47–50.

CONCEPTS OR EXAMPLES

- ☐ Attitudes
- ☐ Work attitudes
- ☐ Attitude object
- ☐ Negative work attitude

- ☐ Parts of attitude (cognitive, affective, behavioral intentions)
- ☐ Attitudes and behavior
- ☐ Positive work attitude

ANALYSIS

_____

_____

_____

_____

_____

_____

_____

_____

_____

PERSONAL REACTIONS

_____

_____

_____

_____

_____

_____

_____

_____

_____

Clockwatchers

Color, 1997
Running Time: 1 hour, 32 minutes
Rating: PG-13
Director: Jill Sprecher
Distributor: Fox Lorber

Four temporary office workers have mind-numbing, routine jobs. The company's full-time workers disdainfully treat them as low status workers. They quickly form close friendships that help them cope with their routine tasks and work environment. This occasionally funny film is a bitingly satirical look at the world of work.

SCENES

DVD CHAPTER 1. OPENING CREDITS TO CHAPTER 2. LOUISE'S DESK (0:02:14–0:05:59)

These scenes begin the film after the opening credits. They start with Iris (Toni Collette) waiting for her supervisor to get her and give her instructions. Barbara (Debra Jo Rupp) approaches Iris while saying, "I can't believe you've been waiting for two hours. Why didn't you say something?" These scenes end with Iris repeatedly stamping "Urgent" on envelopes. The film cuts to Iris boarding a bus.

WHAT TO WATCH FOR AND ASK YOURSELF

- What is the level of organizational commitment of these workers?
- Do they appear satisfied or dissatisfied with their jobs?
- Do they have high job involvement?

CONCEPTS OR EXAMPLES

- ☐ Routine work
- ☐ Worker attitudes
- ☐ Organizational commitment
- ☐ Job involvement

- ☐ Job satisfaction
- ☐ Job dissatisfaction
- ☐ Attitudes and behavior

ANALYSIS

_____

_____

_____

_____

_____

_____

_____

_____

_____

PERSONAL REACTIONS

_____

_____

_____

_____

_____

_____

_____

_____

_____

_____

Office Space

Color, 1999
Running Time: 1 hour, 39 minutes
Rating: R
Director: Mike Judge
Distributor: 20th Century Fox Home Entertainment

This biting satire looks at modern American corporate life through the eyes of three computer programmers. Peter Gibbons (Ron Livingston) is a computer programmer with less than positive feelings about his company, Initech. He and his coworkers develop a way of getting back at the company. This film is director Mike Judge's live-action debut. Judge created the television series *Beavis and Butthead*.[51]

Office Space features a red Swingline® stapler, a favorite of the character Milton (Stephen Root). At the time of the film's making, Swingline did not manufacture a red stapler. A prop designer custom painted a stapler for the film, leading to an almost cult-like following for that color. Early in 2002, Swingline introduced its Rio Red stapler, but only available through its website.[52]

SCENES

DVD CHAPTER 1. ROAD RAGE TO CHAPTER 3. A CASE OF THE MONDAYS (0:00:27–0:08:12)

This sequence begins the film after the black title screen "Twentieth Century Fox Presents." It starts with a shot of a crowded highway during morning rush hour traffic. The scenes end after Bill Lumbergh's (Gary Cole) secretary Peggy (Barbara George-Reiss) says, "Uh-oh. Sounds like somebody's got a case of the Mondays." Peter stares at Samir (Ajay Naidu) and Michael (David Herman). The film cuts to the three programmers having coffee at Chotchkie's. Some R-rated language occurs early in these scenes.

WHAT TO WATCH FOR AND ASK YOURSELF

- What aspects of Peter's behavior show his negative attitudes about working at Initech?
- How does he feel about his supervisors?
- Do his coworkers share his negative feelings? What is the evidence in the scenes?

---

[51] Craddock, *VideoHound's Golden Movie Retriever*, 752.
[52] G. A. Fowler, "Hollywood Ending: Stapler Becomes a Star," *The Wall Street Journal* (July 2, 2002), B1, B4.

CONCEPTS OR EXAMPLES

☐ Work attitudes   ☐ Supervisory satisfaction

☐ Organizational commitment   ☐ Job involvement

☐ Job satisfaction   ☐ Attitudes toward coworkers

☐ Behavioral reaction to attitudes
(behavioral intention)

ANALYSIS

_____

_____

_____

_____

_____

_____

_____

_____

_____

_____

PERSONAL REACTIONS

_____

_____

_____

_____

_____

_____

_____

_____

_____

_____

The Guilt Trip

Color, 2012
Running Time: 1 hour, 35 minutes
Rating: PG-13
Director: Anne Fletcher
Distributor: Paramount Home Entertainment

Andrew Brewster (Seth Rogan) visits his mother Joyce Brewster (Barbara Streisand) and invites her on a 3,000 mile cross-country road trip. His goal is to market his new invention, Scieoclean, a micro-emulsion suspension cleaning product. There almost constant time together forges a strong bond between them which holds for the entire film.

SCENES

DVD CHAPTER 4 (0:18:20–0:21:26)

These scenes begin with Joyce serving Andrew his breakfast. They follow the scenes of Andrew trying to contact Adam Scott (Andrew Margolis, Jr,), Joyce's first love. She comments about her concern for his health. The scenes end after she says she must pack and Andrew must fill her in on the weather in all the states they will go through.

WHAT TO WATCH FOR AND ASK YOURSELF

- How do you characterize Joyce's attitudes?
- How do you characterize Andrew's attitudes?
- Do you expect them to be compatible on their long trans-continental trip?

Joseph E. Champoux

CONCEPTS OR EXAMPLES

- ☐ Attitude
- ☐ Attitude change
- ☐ Cognitive dissonance (internal tension because of conflicting beliefs about an attitude object)
- ☐ Persuasive communication
- ☐ Social influence

ANALYSIS

_____

_____

_____

_____

_____

_____

_____

_____

_____

PERSONAL REACTIONS

_____

_____

_____

_____

_____

_____

_____

_____

_____

CHAPTER 9

Personality

Undoubtedly, you have used or heard phrases such as "That person has an outgoing personality" or "That person has a pleasant personality." **Personality** is a set of traits, characteristics, and predispositions of a person.[53] Personality usually matures and stabilizes by about age 30.[54] The collection of factors that make up an individual's personality affects how that person adjusts to different environments.[55]

Personality psychologists largely agree that five dimensions can describe human personality.[56] The following are typical traits associated with high and low characteristics of each **Big Five Personality** dimension[57]:

1. Extroversion   talkative — quiet
2. Emotional stability   relaxed — anxious
3. Agreeableness   cooperative — rude
4. Conscientiousness   thorough — careless
5. Openness to experience   broad-minded — conventional

[53] Gordon W. Allport, *Personality: A Psychological Interpretation* (New York: Henry Holt, 1937), 24–25.

[54] Robert R. McCrae and Paul T. Costa Jr., "The Stability of Personality: Observations and Evaluations," *Current Directions in Psychological Science* 3, no. 6 (1994): 173–75.

[55] Mark Snyder and William Ickes, "Personality and Social Behavior," in *Handbook of Social Psychology*, vol. 2, ed. Gardner Lindzey and Elliot Aronson (New York: Random House, 1985), 883–947.

[56] John M. Digman, "Personality Structure: Emergence of the Five-Factor Model," *Annual Review of Psychology*, 41 (1990): 417–40; Jerry S. Wiggins and Aaron L. Pincus, "Personality: Structure and Assessment," in *Annual Review of Psychology*, 43, ed. Mark R. Rosensweig and Lyman W. Porter (Stanford, CA: Annual Reviews, 1992), 473–504.

[57] Murray R. Barrick and Michael K. Mount, "The Big Five Personality Dimensions and Job Performance: A Meta-Analysis," *Personnel Psychology*, 44, no. 1 (1991): 1–26; Michael K. Mount, Murray R. Barrick, and J. Perkins Strauss, "Validity of Observer Ratings of the Big Five Personality Factors," *Journal of Applied Psychology* 72, no. 2 (1994): 272–80.

The following films have scenes that show different aspects of personality:

- *Broadcast News*
- *The Odd Couple*
- *The Truth about Cats & Dogs*
- *Who Framed Roger Rabbit*

Some opening scenes from *Broadcast News* show selected aspects of personality development. Scenes from *The Odd Couple* show sharp personality contrasts. *The Truth about Cats & Dogs* offers some humorous scenes showing still another personality. *Who Framed Roger Rabbit* has some exceptionally funny scenes that help one assess Roger's personality.

Broadcast News (I)

Color, 1987
Running Time: 2 hours, 12 minutes
Rating: R
Director: James L. Brooks
Distributor: 20ᵗʰ Century Fox Home Entertainment

This romantic comedy features three well-defined and sharply different personalities. The opening scenes show their early personality development within their families.

Each character has different personality characteristics. Jane Craig (Holly Hunter), a bright, driven, compulsive news producer; Tom Grunich (William Hurt), a smooth, modern news anchor; and Aaron Altman (Albert Brooks), a veteran reporter who reacts jealously to Tom's on-camera success. The romantic triangle among these characters adds a strong comedic flavor to the film.

**Note: Chapter 12 "Motivation: Need Theories" and Chapter 22
"Stress in Organizations" also discuss scenes from this film.**

SCENES

DVD CHAPTER 1. THE EARLY YEARS TO CHAPTER 2. MAIN TITLES (0:00:20–0:05:43)

These scenes start at the beginning of the film after the text screen, "A Gracie Films Production." The scenes open with a shot of the front of the Heart in Hand Restaurant. They end as Jane enters her apartment building. The film cuts to Jane sitting on her bed dialing the telephone.

WHAT TO WATCH FOR AND ASK YOURSELF

- What are the personality dimensions or personality types of these three young people?
- Do you expect their personalities to stay the same when they mature?
- What elements of their family upbringing likely affected their personality development?

CONCEPTS OR EXAMPLES

☐ Personality

☐ Personality development

☐ Type A personality

☐ Type B personality

☐ Extroversion

☐ Openness to experience

ANALYSIS

_____

_____

_____

_____

_____

_____

_____

_____

_____

_____

PERSONAL REACTIONS

_____

_____

_____

_____

_____

_____

_____

_____

_____

The Odd Couple (I)

Color, 1967
Running Time: 1 hour, 46 minutes
Rating: G
Director: Gene Saks
Distributor: Paramount Home Video

Divorced sportswriter Oscar Madison (Walter Matthau) lets his about-to-become divorced best friend Felix Ungar (Jack Lemmon) move into his eight room New York City apartment. They are entirely mismatched. Oscar is disorganized and sloppy; Felix is controlled and tidy. Many interactions center on the Friday night poker game with their circle of friends. This delightfully funny film traces their interactions as Felix gets closer to his divorce and Oscar yearns to live alone again.

**Note: Chapter 12 "Motivation: Need Theories" and Chapter 16
"Conflict in Organizations" also discuss scenes from this film.**

SCENES

There are two sets of scenes at different points in the film. These scenes offer separate character studies of Oscar Madison and Felix Ungar.

DVD CHAPTER 2. POKER NIGHT (0:11:56–0:15:25)

Oscar Madison: This sequence starts as Oscar kicks open the kitchen door and enters the room carrying a tray of food and drinks. It follows the start of card playing by the four players. The sequence ends after Oscar says goodbye to his son Brucie (uncredited)

DVD CHAPTER 7. FOUR MINUTES OF POKER TO CHAPTER 8. BREAK THE LOUSY CUP (0:46:38–0:51:15)

Felix Ungar: These scenes start as Murray (Herb Edelman) rings the bell of Oscar's apartment. They follow Felix's telephone conversation with Oscar while Oscar is covering a baseball game. They end after Murray and Vinnie (John Fiedler) leave the apartment with Vinnie saying, "Some life those playboys got."

WHAT TO WATCH FOR AND ASK YOURSELF

- What personality characteristics do Oscar and Felix show?
- Which personality type or types best describe them?
- What behavior in the scenes helps form your conclusions?

CONCEPTS OR EXAMPLES

- ☐ Personality
- ☐ Personality type
- ☐ Personality characteristics
- ☐ Extroversion-introversion
- ☐ Type A personality

- ☐ Agreeableness
- ☐ Conscientiousness
- ☐ Openness to experience
- ☐ Emotional stability
- ☐ Type B personality

ANALYSIS

_____

_____

_____

_____

_____

_____

_____

_____

_____

_____

PERSONAL REACTIONS

_____

_____

_____

_____

_____

_____

_____

_____

_____

The Truth about Cats & Dogs

Color, 1996
Running Time: 1 hour, 37 minutes
Rating: PG-13
Director: Michael Lehmann
Distributor: 20th Century Fox Home Entertainment

British photographer Brian (Ben Chaplin) has trouble with a photographic session of a large dog on roller skates. He calls Dr. Abby Barnes (Janeane Garafalo), a veterinarian radio talk show host, for advice. Brian falls in love with her voice and invites her for a blind date. Abby is dark haired and short but describes herself as tall and blond, the description of her neighbor Noelle (Uma Thurman). Chaplin's role in this film was his first major American film role.[58]

SCENES

DVD CHAPTER 3. HANK ON WHEELS (0:05:44–0:10:18)

These scenes start with a shot of meters on a machine. A female caller's (Mary Lynn Rajskub) voice-over says, "Hullo. My fish? Uhm, he's depressed and my vet said to bring in a blood sample …" A camera pans to Abby on the air. These scenes follow Abby relaxing in her apartment with her cat. She also has met Roy (James McCaffrey), Noelle's date, who mistakenly rang her bell. The scenes end after Abby says, "And, Brian? … I forgive you." The film cuts to Brian in his studio taking more photographs of Hank (Hank the Dog).

WHAT TO WATCH FOR AND ASK YOURSELF

- What personality type best describes Abby?
- Which personality characteristics does she show?
- What behavior in the scenes helps form your conclusions?

---

[58] N. Vecchiarelli, "Greek Chic," *Premiere* (April 2002): 23–24.

Joseph E. Champoux

CONCEPTS OR EXAMPLES

- ☐ Personality
- ☐ Personality type
- ☐ Big Five personality dimensions
- ☐ Extroversion

- ☐ Introversion
- ☐ Type A personality
- ☐ Type B personality
- ☐ Locus of control (internal, external)

ANALYSIS

_____

_____

_____

_____

_____

_____

_____

_____

_____

_____

PERSONAL REACTIONS

_____

_____

_____

_____

_____

_____

_____

_____

_____

_____

_____

Who Framed Roger Rabbit

Color, 1988
Running Time: 1 hour, 44 minutes
Rating: PG
Director: Robert Zemeckis
Distributor: Touchstone Home Video

This film, which won four Academy Awards, combines animation and live-action to present a 1940s Hollywood in which cartoon characters ('toons) have a life of their own. Roger Rabbit (voiced by Charles Fleischer) becomes the prime suspect in the murder of R. K. Maroon (Alan Tilvern), head of the Maroon Cartoons studio. Roger hires 'toon-hating private detective Eddie Valiant (Bob Hoskins). While investigating, Valiant stumbles onto a conspiracy to destroy all 'toons.[59]

Freddie Prinze Jr. says this film changed his life. His reaction to Roger after seeing the film for the first time included the exclamation, "That guy is living my dream!"[60]

SCENES

DVD CHAPTER 7. ROGER FINDS EDDIE (0:35:44–0:41:10)

These scenes start after Eddie Valiant returns to his office and has his hallway discussion with Baby Herman (voiced by Lou Hirsch). They follow his meeting with Vile Judge Doom (Christopher Lloyd) where he discovers how easily Doom can kill a 'toon. Valiant enters his office and closes the door. The scenes end after Valiant says to Roger, "What's all this 'we' stuff. They just want the rabbit." The film cuts to gunshots blasting off the doorknob and the weasels entering.

WHAT TO WATCH FOR AND ASK YOURSELF

- Which Big Five personality dimensions best describe Roger?
- Is he a Type A personality? Why?
- Which dimensions of the Myers-Briggs Type Indicator® (MBTI) best describe Roger's personality?[61]

---

[59] From CHAMPOUX ICO. *Organizational Behavior*, 1e. © 2001 South-Western, a part of Cengage Learning, Inc. Reproduced by permission. www.cengage.com/permissions

[60] S. Brodner, "The Movie That Changed My Life," *Premiere* (July 2002): 72.

[61] The Myers-Briggs Type Indicator® is a popular personality assessment device that assigns people to one of sixteen personality types based on four bi-polar dimensions. Those dimensions include Extroversion-introversion, among others. See Joseph E. Champoux, *Organizational Behavior: Integrating Individuals, Groups, and Organizations*, 4e (New York: Taylor & Francis, 2011), Ch. 5) for more information about personality and the MBTI.

CONCEPTS OR EXAMPLES

☐ Agreeableness   ☐ Type A personality

☐ Extroversion   ☐ Extroversion-introversion

☐ Openness to experience   ☐ Sensing-intuitive

☐ Emotional stability   ☐ Thinking-feeling

☐ Conscientiousness   ☐ Perceiving-judging

ANALYSIS

_____

_____

_____

_____

_____

_____

_____

_____

_____

PERSONAL REACTIONS

_____

_____

_____

_____

_____

_____

_____

_____

CHAPTER 10
Organizational Culture

Organizational culture is a complex and deep aspect of organizations that can strongly affect organization members.[62] **Organizational culture** includes the values, norms, rites, rituals, ceremonies, heroes, and scoundrels in an organization's history.[63] It defines the content of what a new employee needs to learn to become an accepted organization member.[64]

Organizational cultures divide into multiple **subcultures** that grow readily within an organization's departments, divisions, and operating locations. Different occupational groups also form different subcultures, often with a distinct jargon.

People can view organizational culture at three different but related levels. **Artifacts** are the most visible part of an organization's culture. They are the obvious features of an organization such as sounds, architecture, smells, stories, behavior, attire, and language. **Values**, the next level of awareness, tell organization members what they "ought" to do in various situations. **Basic assumptions**, an almost invisible level of organizational culture, are another form of values. Veteran organization members often are not consciously aware of basic assumptions.

Organizational culture concepts appear subtly in some films, boldly in others. The following films offer both possibilities.

- *Top Gun*
- *The Godfather*
- *Dead Poets Society*
- *The Hunt for Red October*

---

[62] Mats Alvesson and Per-Olof Berg, *Corporate Culture and Organizational Symbolism*, (New York: Hawthorne/Walter de Gruyter, 1992); Edgar H. Schein, "Coming to a New Awareness of Organizational Culture," *Sloan Management Review* 25, no. 1 (1984): 3–16; Edgar H. Schein, *Organizational Culture and Leadership*, 4th ed. (San Francisco: Jossey-Bass, 2010).

[63] Terrence E. Deal and Allan A. Kennedy, *Corporate Cultures: The Rites and Rituals of Corporate Life* (Reading, MA: Addison-Wesley, 1982).

[64] Joanne Martin, *Organizational Culture: Mapping the Terrain* (Thousand Oaks, CA: Sage Publications, Inc., 2002); Benjamin Schneider, Mark G. Ehrhart, and William H. Macey, "Organizational Climate and Culture," *Annual Review of Psychology* 64, no. 1 (2013): 361–88; Harrison Miller Trice and Janice M. Beyer, *The Cultures of Work Organizations* (Englewood Cliffs, NJ: Prentice Hall, 1993), chap. 1.

Top Gun boldly shows some obvious aspects of organizational culture. The opening scenes of *The Godfather* show some subtle, often hidden, aspects. *Dead Poets Society* shows obvious aspects of an organization's culture in a nonmilitary setting. *The Hunt for Red October* has a short scene showing the role of stories in an organization's culture.

Top Gun

Color, 1986
Running Time: 1 hour, 40 minutes
Rating: PG
Director: Tony Scott
Distributor: Paramount Home Video

This action-based film simply screams with aspects of U.S. naval aviation culture. Part of the film focuses on the relationship between Lt. Pete Mitchell (call sign Maverick, Tom Cruise) and sultry civilian instructor Charlotte Blackwood (call sign Charlie, Kelly McGillis). Many scenes throughout the film show several aspects of naval aviation culture in action. The use of real U.S. Navy people and equipment at various places gives a strong sense of reality.

SCENES

DVD CHAPTER 1. OPENING CREDITS TO CHAPTER 2. DANGER ZONE (0:00:00–0:04:06)

This sequence begins with the Paramount logo and background music followed by the opening title credits. Closely watch the action behind the credits. The scenes behind the credits were shot on a U.S. Navy aircraft carrier using U.S. Navy people, not actors and actresses. This sequence ends with a wide shot of an aircraft carrier. The text on the screen reads, "Indian Ocean. Present Day." These scenes complement the more subtle scenes showing basic assumptions from *The Godfather* (pp. 89-90).

WHAT TO WATCH FOR AND ASK YOURSELF

- What artifacts or physical characteristics of U.S. Naval aviation culture do the scenes show?
- Are any subcultures shown in the scenes? If *yes*, what defines the subcultures?
- What values do you infer from the scenes?

CONCEPTS OR EXAMPLES

- ☐ Dimensions of organizational culture
- ☐ Levels of organizational culture (artifacts, values, basic assumptions)
- ☐ Perspectives on organizational culture
- ☐ Cultural symbolism
- ☐ Functions of organizational culture
- ☐ Dysfunctions of organizational culture
- ☐ Basic assumptions

ANALYSIS

_____

_____

_____

_____

_____

_____

_____

_____

PERSONAL REACTIONS

_____

_____

_____

_____

_____

_____

_____

_____

The Godfather (II)

Color, 1972
Running Time: 2 hours, 51 minutes
Rating: R
Director: Francis Ford Coppola
Distributor: Paramount Home Video

This film, based on Mario Puzo's novel, is a powerful look at a Mafia family led by Don Corleone (Marlon Brando). It is an intense film that roams through the personal lives of its characters and shows the fiercely violent side of organized crime. The film suggests stunning parallels between managing a gangster organization and managing an organization of any other type. An irresistible work, *The Godfather* is filled with memorable scenes and memorable performances. The American Film Institute in 1998 ranked this film in the top 100 American films.[65]

Note: Chapter 6 "Ethics and Behavior in Organizations" and Chapter 21 "Power and Political Behavior" also discuss scenes from this film.

SCENES

DVD CHAPTER 1. I BELIEVE IN AMERICA (0:00:47–0:07:01)

These scenes start after the opening titles with Bonasera (Salvatore Corsitto) the undertaker's voice-over, "I believe in America." The film opens on his face as he continues to speak. These scenes end after Don Corleone says to Tom Hagen (Robert Duvall), "I mean, we're not murderers in spite of what this undertaker says." Don Corleone sniffs his lapel flower. The film cuts to the wedding reception.

WHAT TO WATCH FOR AND ASK YOURSELF

- What levels of this organization's culture appear in these scenes?
- Do the scenes show any values or basic assumptions that guide behavior in this culture?
- Is the culture functional or dysfunctional for this organization?

---

[65] Craddock, *VideoHound's Golden Movie Retriever*, 429.

CONCEPTS OR EXAMPLES

☐ Organizational culture   ☐ Artifacts/physical characteristics

☐ Values   ☐ Espoused values

☐ Basic assumptions   ☐ In-use values

ANALYSIS

_____

_____

_____

_____

_____

_____

_____

_____

_____

PERSONAL REACTIONS

_____

_____

_____

_____

_____

_____

_____

_____

_____

Dead Poets Society

Color, 1989
Running Time: 2 hours, 8 minutes
Rating: PG
Director: Peter Weir
Distributor: Buena Vista Home Entertainment

Charismatic English teacher John Keating (Robin Williams) tries to unleash the creativity and individuality of his young New England preparatory school students. Staid headmaster Nolan (Norman Lloyd) does not always accept their behavior. The school's administration eventually dismisses Keating because they believe he too powerfully affects student behavior.

SCENES

DVD CHAPTER 2. OPENING CREDITS (0:00:29–0:04:20)

These scenes start at the beginning of the film after the title screen "A STEVEN HAFT PRODUCTION IN ASSOCIATION WITH WITT-THOMAS PRODUCTIONS". They end after the introduction of Mr. Keating. He sits down and the film cuts to an outside scene.

WHAT TO WATCH FOR AND ASK YOURSELF

- What are some physical artifacts of the school's organizational culture?
- What are some of this culture's dominant values?
- What is the function of rites and rituals in this situation?

CONCEPTS OR EXAMPLES

- ☐ Organizational culture
- ☐ Rites and rituals
- ☐ Artifacts/physical characteristics
- ☐ Values
- ☐ Basic assumptions
- ☐ Levels of organizational culture

ANALYSIS

_____

_____

_____

_____

_____

_____

_____

_____

_____

PERSONAL REACTIONS

_____

_____

_____

_____

_____

_____

_____

_____

_____

_____

The Hunt for Red October (I)

Color, 1990
Running Time: 2 hours, 15 minutes
Rating: PG
Director: John McTiernan
Distributor: Paramount Pictures

This film is an intense story of the search for the Soviet submarine *Red October*. Contradictory information says its commander Captain Marko Ramius (Sean Connery) is either defecting to the United States or has gone berserk and will unleash nuclear missiles on the U.S. The Soviets want the U.S. to find the *Red October* and destroy it. CIA agent Dr. Jack Ryan (Alec Baldwin) believes Ramius wants to defect and does not want him killed.

Note: Chapter 23 "Organizational Design" also discusses scenes from this film.

SCENES

DVD CHAPTER 1 TURBULENCE (0:09:46–0:12:45)

The scenes start with a dark screen and the growling sound of a submerged submarine. It slowly emerges from the dark screen. These scenes follow the meeting between CIA agent Jack Ryan and Admiral Greer (James Earl Jones). The scenes end as Seaman Jones (Courtney B. Vance) takes the sonar alarm and says, "Conn. Sonar. New contact, bearing 0-niner-7. Designate contact number Sierra-3-5." The film cuts to the conning tower and a shot of the loudspeaker. Jones' reference to "COB" means Chief of the Boat (Chief Watson, Larry Ferguson).

WHAT TO WATCH FOR AND ASK YOURSELF

- In what level of an organization's culture do stories reside?
- Does the story convey any organizational values?
- What role does the story play in this situation?

CONCEPTS OR EXAMPLES

☐ Values

☐ Basic assumptions

☐ Artifacts/physical characteristics

☐ Levels of organizational culture

☐ Accuracy

☐ Stories

ANALYSIS

_____

_____

_____

_____

_____

_____

_____

_____

_____

PERSONAL REACTIONS

_____

_____

_____

_____

_____

_____

_____

_____

CHAPTER 11

Organizational Socialization

Organizational socialization is a powerful process by which people learn an organization's culture.[66] It affects individual behavior and helps shape and maintain the organization's culture.[67] Organizational socialization happens in three stages. The product of one stage becomes the input to the next stage.

Choice: anticipatory socialization is the first socialization stage a person experiences. This stage happens before a person joins an organization or takes a new job in the same or different organization. The anticipatory stage builds expectations about what it is like to work for the organization. The **entry/encounter** stage follows the choice stage, starting after crossing the organization's boundary. A new employee learns whether his or her expectations match the reality of organization life.[68]

Change happens during the entry/encounter stage, as it flows and blends into the **metamorphosis** stage. If a new employee has successfully resolved the demands from multiple socialization sources, he or she begins to feel comfortable in the new role.[69]

The following films have scenes with a range of portrayals of organizational socialization:

- *The Firm*
- *The Hudsucker Proxy*
- *An Officer and a Gentleman*
- *Snow White and the Seven Dwarfs*

---

66   J. Steven Ott, *The Organizational Culture Perspective* (Pacific Grove, CA: Brooks/Cole, 1989); Schein, *Organizational Culture and Leadership*; Trice and Beyer, *Cultures of Work Organizations*.

67   Michael W. Kramer, *Organizational Socialization: Joining and Leaving Organizations* (Cambridge, UK: Polity Press, 2010); John Van Maanen and Edgar H. Schein, "Toward a Theory of Organizational Socialization," in *Research in Organizational Behavior,* vol. 1., ed. Barry M. Staw and Larry L. Cummings (Greenwich, CT: JAI Press, 1979), 209–64; Connie R. Wanberg, ed., *The Oxford Handbook of Organizational Socialization* (New York: Oxford University Press, Inc., 2012).

68   C. Fisher, "Organizational Socialization: An Integrative Review," in *Research in Personnel and Human Resource Management*, vol. 4, ed. Kendrith M. Rowland and Gerald R. Ferris (Greenwich, CT: JAI Press, 1986), 101–45; Van Maanen and Schein, "Theory of Organizational Socialization," 209–64.

69   John Van Maanen and Edgar H. Schein, "Career Development," in *Improving Life at Work: Behavioral Science Approaches to Organizational Change*, ed. J. Richard Hackman and J. Lloyd Suttle (Santa Monica: CA: Goodyear Publishing Company, 1977), chap. 2.

The opening scenes from *The Firm* show early socialization stages. Scenes from *The Hudsucker Proxy* humorously present a new employee's first encounter with an organization. *An Officer and a Gentleman* is more serious. It shows the transformation of new recruits into U.S. Naval officers. The transformation of the Queen to an old woman in *Snow White and the Seven Dwarfs* shows the results of the metamorphosis stage, with strong symbolic characterization.

The Firm

Color, 1993
Running Time: 2 hours, 34 minutes
Rating: R
Director: Sydney Pollack
Distributor: Paramount Pictures

Mitch McDeere (Tom Cruise) graduates from Harvard Law School with honors and in the top five of his class. Many top law firms vigorously recruit him. Mitch chooses a small Memphis, Tennessee firm with a large starting salary, a new Mercedes, and a low-interest home mortgage. He quickly learns that "The Firm" is entangled in a web of murder and corruption.[70]

SCENES

DVD CHAPTER 1. OPENING CREDITS TO CHAPTER 3. THE FAMILY (0:00:19–0:12:20)

This sequence begins the film after the Paramount logo and a black screen. It opens with a panning shot of Cambridge, Massachusetts across the Charles River. The opening sequence includes the film credits. This sequence ends as Mitch and Abby (Jeanne Tripplehorn) embrace after their discussion about accepting the firm's offer. The film cuts to Oliver Lambert's (Hal Holbrook) office and a discussion about Abby's telephone calls while in Memphis. The discussion continues about the status of Hodges and Kozinski, two members of the firm.

WHAT TO WATCH FOR AND ASK YOURSELF

- What expectations does Mitch develop during the anticipatory socialization stage?
- What expectations does Abby develop during their Memphis visit?
- Does she fully share her expectations with Mitch?

---

[70]   Champoux, "Seeing and Valuing Diversity," 310–16.

Joseph E. Champoux

CONCEPTS OR EXAMPLES

- ☐ Role episodes (role sender(s), focal person, sent role, received role)
- ☐ Role behavior (pivotal, relevant, peripheral)

- ☐ Expectations
- ☐ Anticipatory stage of socialization
- ☐ Socialization processes (recruiting, recruitment interviews)

ANALYSIS

_____
_____
_____
_____
_____
_____
_____
_____
_____

PERSONAL REACTIONS

_____
_____
_____
_____
_____
_____
_____
_____
_____
_____

The Hudsucker Proxy (I)

Color, 1994
Running Time: 1 hour, 51 minutes
Rating: PG
Director: Joel Coen
Distributor: Warner Home Video

Norville Barnes (Tim Robbins), a graduate of the Muncie College of Business Administration, quickly moves from mailroom clerk to president of Hudsucker Industries. The board of directors appoints him in the hope that his incompetence will drive down the stock price so they can buy a controlling interest. Norville has his own idea for a product, a simple plastic hoop. After a slow start in sales, the hula hoop becomes a success, drives the stock price up, and causes the board great distress. Sidney J. Mussburger (Paul Newman) aspires to the presidency and sabotages Norville by presenting him as insane. The film takes a delightful twist at the end. Norville inherits the late Waring Hudsucker's (Charles Durning) fortune, regains the presidency, and presents the board with a new product idea—the Frisbee®.

Note: Chapter 23 "Organizational Design" also discusses scenes from this film.

SCENES

DVD CHAPTER 5 MAILROOM ORIENTATION. THROUGH CHAPTER 7 BLUE LETTER ALERT. (0:13:03–0:17:42)

These scenes start as Norville enters the mailroom pushing his mail basket and listening to directions from the Mail Room Orienter (Christopher Darga). They follow Sidney J. Mussburger's presentation to the board of his idea to appoint an idiot as president. These scenes end after Norville receives the blue letter to deliver. The film cuts to an opening elevator door.

WHAT TO WATCH FOR AND ASK YOURSELF

- Which stage of socialization is Norville experiencing?
- What are the sources of Norville's socialization experiences?
- Which role behavior does he learn: pivotal, relevant, or peripheral?

CONCEPTS OR EXAMPLES

- ☐ Organizational socialization
- ☐ Entry/encounter stage
- ☐ Sources of socialization (supervisors, coworkers)

- ☐ Sense-making process (change, contrast, surprise)
- ☐ Pivotal role behavior
- ☐ Peripheral role behavior
- ☐ Relevant role behavior

ANALYSIS

_____

_____

_____

_____

_____

_____

_____

_____

_____

_____

PERSONAL REACTIONS

_____

_____

_____

_____

_____

_____

_____

_____

_____

_____

An Officer and a Gentleman

Color, 1982
Running Time: 2 hours, 6 minutes
Rating: R
Director: Taylor Hackford
Distributor: Paramount Home Video

This film powerfully shows the training regimen of the Navy Officer Candidate School. Zack Mayo (Richard Gere) and other officer candidates experience near torture at the hands of their drill instructor, Gunnery Sergeant Emil Foley (Louis Gossett, Jr.). Zack, a loner, learns about discipline and dependence on others for success. The film is rich in scenes showing socialization experiences. It has a dramatic, rough portrayal of the entry/encounter socialization stage. The film has several instances of strong language and strong sexual references. This film ranked 29th in the 2002 American Film Institute rankings of cinema love stories.[71]

SCENES

There are two sets of scenes. The first set shows socialization experiences shortly after starting Officer Candidate School. The second shows the finished product at graduation after thirteen weeks of training.

DVD CHAPTER 4. BASIC TRAINING (0:21:12–0:28:08)

Set 1 starts with a shot of Sergeant Foley's candidates running through water and singing. It follows the scene near the officer's club of Foley pushing Mayo and Sid Worley (David Keith) to do more pushups. The set ends after Casey Seegar (Lisa Eilbacher) fails to scale the wall. Foley says, "Ahh! Walk around. Walk around, sugar britches." The film cuts to a classroom scene.

DVD CHAPTER 14. AN OFFICER... (1:54:45–1:58:36)

The graduation ceremony begins the second set of scenes with the entire platoon assembled at attention in white uniforms. This set follows the fight between Mayo and Foley. It ends after the last graduate, Emiliano Della Serra (Tony Plana), gives Foley a silver dollar and returns his salute. The film cuts to a shot of Mayo riding his motorcycle while wearing his white dress uniform.

WHAT TO WATCH FOR AND ASK YOURSELF

- What is the purpose of debasement experiences during officer candidate training?
- What are some likely results?
- Are these results functional or dysfunctional for all involved?

---

[71] Germain, "'Casablanca' Top Romance Film," C13.

CONCEPTS OR EXAMPLES

☐ Socialization process
☐ Entry/encounter stage
☐ Debasement experiences

☐ New self-image
☐ Metamorphosis stage

ANALYSIS

_____

_____

_____

_____

_____

_____

_____

_____

_____

_____

PERSONAL REACTIONS

_____

_____

_____

_____

_____

_____

_____

_____

_____

Snow White and the Seven Dwarfs

Color, 1937
Running Time: 1 hour, 24 minutes
Rating: G
Director: David Hand
Distributor: Buena Vista Home Entertainment

Walt Disney's pioneering first feature-length animated film adapts the famous Brothers Grimm fairy tale. The studio developed new animation techniques to get smooth character movement. For more realism, Disney hired live actors as models.[72] *Snow White* features many memorable songs including "Whistle While You Work."

The jealous Queen (voiced by Lucille La Verne), Snow White's stepmother, fears Snow White's beauty. She transforms herself into an old woman and convinces Snow White (voiced by Adriana Caselotti) to eat a poisoned apple. Snow White falls into the Sleeping Death. Her Seven Dwarf friends try to protect her in their forest house and stand watch over her sleep.[73]

SCENES

DVD CHAPTER 17 THE QUEEN PREPARES A DISGUISE (0:49:17–0:52:03)

The scenes start as the Queen learns that Snow White is alive. She now wants to create a way to kill her. They end after the Queen's transformation into the old woman. She leers at the camera, the screen goes black, and the film cuts to the Seven Dwarfs' house where everyone is singing.

WHAT TO WATCH FOR AND ASK YOURSELF

- Does the Queen's transformation into the old woman symbolically show the result of the metamorphosis socialization stage?
- Can metamorphosis in organizational socialization have such extreme results in a real setting?
- What types of organizations feature such powerful socialization processes?

---

[72] Craddock, *VideoHound's Golden Film Retriever*, 939; Shamus Culhane, *Talking Animals and Other People* (New York: St. Martin's Press, 1986); Stefan Kanfer, *Serious Business: The Art and Commerce of Animation in America from* Betty Boop *to* Toy Story (New York: Scribner, 1997).

[73] From CHAMPOUX ICO. *Organizational Behavior*, 1e. © 2001 South-Western, a part of Cengage Learning, Inc. Reproduced by permission. www.cengage.com/permissions

Joseph E. Champoux

CONCEPTS OR EXAMPLES

☐ Metamorphosis (transformation)
☐ Symbolism

☐ Result of metamorphosis socialization stage

ANALYSIS

_____
_____
_____
_____
_____
_____
_____
_____
_____
_____

PERSONAL REACTIONS

_____
_____
_____
_____
_____
_____
_____
_____
_____
_____
_____

CHAPTER 12
Motivation: Need Theories

Need theories of motivation propose psychological needs as hypothetical concepts to explain people's behavior. Needs are invisible characteristics of people that help shape their responses to different stimuli or objects in their environment. People vary greatly in need patterns that guide their behavior.[74]

Some common needs are the need for affiliation and the need for achievement. The need for affiliation helps guide a person's social behavior. A person with strong affiliation needs will likely interact with more people than a person with weak affiliation needs. The need for achievement has strong ties to a person's successful work performance. Low achievers typically do not strive for as high a performance level as high achievers.

Some theories propose **need hierarchies** with some needs more important to a person's motivation than other needs. People move up and down their need hierarchy. As they satisfy some needs, they move upward; as they dissatisfy others, they move downward.[75]

The following films, including some animated films, offer scenes showing various aspects of the need theories of motivation:

- *Broadcast News*
- *The Odd Couple*
- *Toy Story*
- *The Many Adventures of Winnie the Pooh*

Broadcast News shows two people with different need structures. Felix Unger and Oscar Madison in *The Odd Couple* have vastly different need structures, making them a true odd couple. *Toy Story* offers a symbolic example of esteem needs, especially Buzz Lightyear's loss of self-esteem. *The Many Adventures of Winnie the Pooh* has funny scenes showing the needs that motivate Tigger.

---

74 Martin G. Evans, "Organizational Behavior: The Central Role of Motivation," in *Yearly Review of Management of the Journal of Management*, ed. Jerry G. Hunt and John D. Blair, 12, no. 2, 1986, 203–22; Craig C. Pinder, *Work Motivation in Organizational Behavior*, 2e (New York: Psychology Press, 2008); Bernard Weiner, *Human Motivation: Metaphors, Theories, and Research* (Newbury Park, CA: Sage Publications, 1992).

75 Clayton P. Alderfer, *Existence, Relatedness, and Growth: Human Needs in Organizational Settings* (New York: Free Press, 1972); Abraham H. Maslow, "A Theory of Human Motivation," *Psychological Review* 50 no. 4 (1943): 370–96; Abraham H. Maslow (with Deborah C. Stephens and Gary Heil.), *Maslow on Management* (New York: John Wiley & Sons, 1998).

Broadcast News (II)

Color, 1987
Running Time: 2 hours, 12 minutes
Rating: R
Director: James L. Brooks
Distributor: 20th Century Fox Home Entertainment

This romantic comedy features three well-defined and sharply different personalities. The opening scenes show their early personality development within their families.

Each character has different personality characteristics. Jane Craig (Holly Hunter), a bright, driven, compulsive news producer; Tom Grunich (William Hurt), a smooth, modern news anchor; and Aaron Altman (Albert Brooks), a veteran reporter who reacts jealously to Tom's on-camera success. The romantic triangle among these characters adds a strong comedic flavor to the film.

Note: Chapter 9 "Personality" and Chapter 22 "Stress in
Organizations" also discuss scenes from this film.

SCENES

DVD CHAPTER 8. CENTRAL AMERICA (0:26:42–0:29:12)

These scenes start with Aaron speaking Spanish to the Nicaraguan guerrilla leader (Luis Valderrama). They follow the stressful editing room scene and Jane's discussion with Tom in the newsroom. The scenes end after Aaron tells Jane he does not feel well. The film cuts to Jane crying while sitting on a pier.

WHAT TO WATCH FOR AND ASK YOURSELF

- What needs motivate Jane?
- What is Aaron's need structure?
- Where is each of them in the hierarchy of needs?

CONCEPTS OR EXAMPLES

- ☐ Needs
- ☐ Motivation
- ☐ Need for recognition
- ☐ E.R.G. theory
- ☐ Enrichment cycle

- ☐ Growth needs
- ☐ Need for achievement
- ☐ Need hierarchy
- ☐ Deficiency cycle

ANALYSIS

_____

_____

_____

_____

_____

_____

_____

_____

_____

PERSONAL REACTIONS

_____

_____

_____

_____

_____

_____

_____

_____

_____

The Odd Couple (II)

Color, 1968
Running Time: 1 hour, 46 minutes
Rating: G
Director: Gene Saks
Distributor: Paramount Home Video

Divorced sportswriter Oscar Madison (Walter Matthau) lets his about-to-become divorced best friend Felix Ungar (Jack Lemmon) move into his eight room New York City apartment. They are entirely mismatched. Oscar is disorganized and sloppy; Felix is controlled and tidy. Many interactions center on the Friday night poker game with their circle of friends. This delightfully funny film traces their interactions as Felix gets closer to his divorce and Oscar yearns to live alone again.

Note: Chapter 9 "Personality" and Chapter 16 "Conflict in Organizations" also discuss scenes from this film.

SCENES

DVD CHAPTER 4. IMPOSSIBLE TO LIVE WITH TO CHAPTER 5. OSCAR'S PROPOSAL (0:34:11–0:40:27)

These scenes, which follow the scene of Felix hyperventilating in Oscar's apartment, begin with Felix and Oscar walking down a street. Oscar is eating an ice-cream cone. They end as Oscar and Felix leave a bench and walk up some stairs. Oscar says to Felix, "You'll go on street corners and cry. They'll throw nickels at you. You'll work, Felix, you'll work." The film fades to Oscar and Felix getting off an elevator in Oscar's apartment building.

WHAT TO WATCH FOR AND ASK YOURSELF

- What needs best fit Felix Ungar's behavior in these scenes?
- What needs best fit Oscar Madison's behavior in these scenes?
- Do they both have the same need patterns? Describe the patterns.

CONCEPTS OR EXAMPLES

- ☐ Need for order
- ☐ Need for affiliation (social needs)
- ☐ Need for achievement

- ☐ Need for autonomy

- ☐ Belongingness and love needs
- ☐ Esteem needs
- ☐ Existence needs (physiological and safety needs)
- ☐ Growth needs

ANALYSIS

_____

_____

_____

_____

_____

_____

_____

_____

_____

PERSONAL REACTIONS

_____

_____

_____

_____

_____

_____

_____

_____

_____

Toy Story

Color, 1995
Running Time: 1 hour, 21 minutes
Rating: G
Director: John Lasseter
Distributor: Warner Home Video

This captivating and emotionally deep story tells what we have always imagined. Toys have a life and social organization of their own when humans are not present.

Andy's (voiced by John Morris) favorite toy is Sheriff Woody (voiced by Tom Hanks). He receives a new toy as a birthday gift, Buzz Lightyear, Space Ranger (voiced by Tim Allen). Buzz's presence disrupts the established social order, especially Woody's senior status among the toys. Concern about continuing as Andy's favorite causes conflict between Woody, Buzz, and the other toys. The tension increases because Buzz thinks he is a real space ranger, not a toy. Watch for the early scene of Mr. Potato Head (voiced by Don Rickles) calling the hockey puck a hockey puck! This is the first computer-animated feature-length film.[76]

SCENES

DVD CHAPTER 23. "BUZZ, I CAN'T DO THIS WITHOUT YOU" (0:56:39–1:00:32)

These scenes start with an outside shot of Sid's (voiced by Erik von Detten) house during a thunderstorm. Woody is trapped under a box and needs Buzz's help to get out. Buzz had earlier seen a television commercial advertising him as a toy, his first sense of not being a real space ranger. The scenes end as Sid's alarm clock rings. It falls to the floor as Sid wakes up.

WHAT TO WATCH FOR AND ASK YOURSELF

- Do Woody and Buzz need each other to solve the problem of getting out of Sid's room?
- What is Buzz's level of self-esteem at this point?
- How does Woody motivate Buzz? Does he improve Buzz's self-esteem? If *yes*, how?

---

[76] From CHAMPOUX ICO. *Organizational Behavior*, 1e. © 2001 South-Western, a part of Cengage Learning, Inc. Reproduced by permission. www.cengage.com/permissions

CONCEPTS OR EXAMPLES

- ☐ Motivation
- ☐ Esteem needs
- ☐ Self-esteem

- ☐ Problem solving
- ☐ Collaborative behavior
- ☐ Self-concept

ANALYSIS

_____

_____

_____

_____

_____

_____

_____

_____

_____

_____

PERSONAL REACTIONS

_____

_____

_____

_____

_____

_____

_____

_____

_____

_____

The Many Adventures of Winnie the Pooh

Color, 1977
Running Time: 1 hour, 53 minutes
Rating: G
Director: John Lounsbery, Wolfgang Reitherman
Distributor: Buena Vista Home Entertainment

Disney's animated presentation of A. A. Milne's charming characters follows them through a series of adventures in the Hundred Acre Wood. Pooh, Piglet, Tigger, Rabbit, and the others offer engaging performances that show different aspects of motivation and needs.[77]

SCENES

DVD CHAPTER 20 POOH IS HAVING A PROBLEM (1:04:14–1:11:27)

These scenes begin with Pooh (voiced by Sterling Holloway) and Piglet (voiced by John Fiedler) following footprints in the snow. They think they belong to "something," perhaps dangerous animals. Pooh hears a sound and sees something in a tree. Pooh says, "Look, look, Piglet, there's something in that tree over there." The scenes end after Tigger's (voiced by Paul Winchell) bouncing and he says, "I'm the only one". Tigger roars. The scene fades to an image of a storybook with a page reading, "Chapter X, *In Which* Christopher Robin and Pooh Come to the Enchanted Place and We Say Good-bye."

WHAT TO WATCH FOR AND ASK YOURSELF

- What needs, in a figurative sense, is Tigger trying to satisfy?
- What needs motivate Rabbit (voiced by Junius Matthews)?
- Observe the changes in Tigger's behavior after he frustrates his needs. Does Tigger change again after he satisfies his basic needs?

---

[77] Champoux, "Animated Films," 79-100; Yvette A. Castro, an engineering graduate student at The University of New Mexico, first nudged me toward *The Many Adventures of Winnie the Pooh* as a source of film scenes.

CONCEPTS OR EXAMPLES

- ☐ Motivation
- ☐ Safety need
- ☐ Need for dominance
- ☐ Need for order

- ☐ "Bouncing need"
- ☐ Belongingness and love needs
- ☐ Need for control

ANALYSIS

_____

_____

_____

_____

_____

_____

_____

_____

_____

PERSONAL REACTIONS

_____

_____

_____

_____

_____

_____

_____

_____

_____

_____

CHAPTER 13

Motivation: Cognitive and Behavioral Theories

Cognitive and behavioral theories of motivation explain human behavior in different ways. **Cognitive theories** use internal psychological processes (cognitions) as their explanation. **Behavioral theories** focus on observable behavior and do not use a cognitive explanation.[78]

There are three cognitive theories. **Expectancy theory** describes internal processes of choice among different behaviors. People will go toward positively valued outcomes if they believe they can get them. **Equity theory** describes how people react when they feel unfairly treated by managers. People compare their ratio of outcomes to inputs to the perceived ratio of another person in the organization. When the ratios are unequal, the person behaves to restore equality (equity). **Goal-setting theory** emphasizes setting external goals that a person tries to reach. Specific, challenging, and reachable goals highly motivate many people.

Behavior modification is a fourth motivation theory that focuses on observable behavior. This theory does not use internal psychological processes to explain human behavior. It assumes people go toward positive outcomes and avoid negative outcomes.

The following films have scenes that show various concepts from the cognitive and behavioral theories of motivation:

- *Dangerous Minds*
- *Hercules*
- *First Kid*
- *Mr. Holland's Opus*

Dangerous Minds offers powerful scenes anchored in expectancy theory and equity theory. The animated *Hercules* cleverly shows how training and skill development reduce a blockage between effort and performance. *First Kid* has live-action scenes that also show training as a way to reduce an individual blockage. *Mr. Holland's Opus* has many examples of motivation and behavior modification.

---

[78]   Evans, "Organizational Behavior," 203–22; Pinder, *Work Motivation*; Weimer, *Human Motivation*.

Dangerous Minds

Color, 1995
Running Time: 1 hour, 39 minutes
Rating: R
Director: John N. Smith
Distributor: Buena Vista Home Entertainment

Former U.S. Marine LouAnne Johnson (Michelle Pfeiffer) accepts a teaching job at a high school that buses in special students. They are inner city students who typically have underachieved academically. Ms. Johnson tries to motivate them to what she perceives as their likely achievement levels. Principal Grandey (Courtney B. Vance) perceives her motivation methods as unorthodox and pressures her to follow the course outlines. The film is based on LouAnne Johnson's autobiography.[79]

SCENES

DVD CHAPTER 9. DYLAN-DYLAN CONTEST (0:53:42–0:58:10)

These scenes start with a shot of the hallway after Principal Grandey reprimanded Johnson for taking students to an amusement park without signed permissions. Johnson's voice-over says, "Angela, would you read the first line?" Ms. Johnson then announces the Dylan-Dylan contest. These scenes end after her students draw prizes from the reward box. The film cuts to Ms. Johnson picking up trash in her classroom. Callie (Idina Harris) enters the classroom. These scenes have a few instances of R-rated language.

WHAT TO WATCH FOR AND ASK YOURSELF

- What methods does Ms. Johnson use to motivate her students to high performance?
- Does her motivation approach change the behavior of these under-performing students?
- Is it fair for her to reward the non-winners by letting them pick from the reward box?

---

[79]   LouAnne Johnson, *My Possé Don't Do Homework* (New York: St. Martin's Press, 1993).

Joseph E. Champoux

CONCEPTS OR EXAMPLES

- ☐ Motivation
- ☐ Expectancy theory
- ☐ Equity theory
- ☐ Perceived negative inequity

- ☐ Extrinsic rewards
- ☐ Intrinsic rewards
- ☐ Ratio of outcomes to inputs
- ☐ Perceived positive inequity

ANALYSIS

_____

_____

_____

_____

_____

_____

_____

_____

PERSONAL REACTIONS

_____

_____

_____

_____

_____

_____

_____

_____

_____

116

Hercules

Color, 1997
Running Time: 1 hour, 33 minutes
Rating: G
Director: Ron Clements, John Musker
Distributor: Buena Vista Home Entertainment

Hades (voiced by James Woods), Lord of the Underworld, wants to overthrow Zeus (voiced by Rip Torn) on Mount Olympus. Because young Hercules, son of Zeus, shows great strength, Hades perceives him as his only blockage. He kidnaps the baby and gives him to a poor family who raise him as a mortal. Hercules (voiced by Tate Donovan) learns of his origin and discovers that he must become a true hero to return to his father and Mount Olympus. Retired Greek hero trainer Philoctetes (Phil) the Satyr (voiced by Danny DeVito) helps Hercules along the way. Disney's version of this Greek myth, of course, lacks the violence and sex of the original story.

SCENES

DVD CHAPTER 10 THE SEARCH FOR PHILOCTETES THROUGH CHAPTER 12 "ONE LAST HOPE" (0:24:22–0:31:49)

This sequence begins with Hercules and Pegasus walking in a forest. Hercules says, "Are you sure this is the right place?" Pegasus nods and grunts. These scenes end after Phil the Satyr says, "Well OK. OK. You want a road test? Saddle up kid. We're going to Thebes!" The three fly off on Pegasus. A woman screams and Phil says, "Sounds like your basic DID, Damsel in Distress."

WHAT TO WATCH FOR AND ASK YOURSELF

- What is Hercules' valence on becoming a true hero? Why?
- Do Phil's activities help Hercules improve his effort-performance expectancy? Why?
- At the end of the scenes, do you believe Hercules is prepared for the challenges ahead? Why?

CONCEPTS OR EXAMPLES

- ☐ Motivation
- ☐ Individual blockages
- ☐ Organizational blockages
- ☐ Skills and abilities

- ☐ Effort-performance expectancy
- ☐ Performance-outcome expectancy
- ☐ Training
- ☐ Valence

ANALYSIS

PERSONAL REACTIONS

First Kid

Color, 1996
Running Time: 1 hour, 51 minutes
Rating: PG
Director: David Mickey Evans
Distributor: Buena Vista Home Entertainment

Secret Service agent Sam Simms (Sinbad) has the thankless job of guarding the President's shielded, frustrated son, Luke Davenport (Brock Pierce). Luke does not like the restrictions he has as the President's son. Sam goes around the rules to help Luke experience what other teenagers experience, causing some comedic and dramatic moments.

SCENES

DVD CHAPTER 6 BOXING LESSONS (0:51:00–0:54:12)

These scenes start with Luke and Sam skipping rope in the gymnasium. They follow Luke and Sam's late night return to the White House after his first round of training. These scenes end as the camera zooms back from the front of the Second Street Gym with everyone applauding. The film cuts to a night shot of the Washington Monument and the dance mixer at Luke's school. These scenes include some intercut moments at Luke's school.

WHAT TO WATCH FOR AND ASK YOURSELF

- What effect will Luke's training have on his effort-performance expectancy in a possible future fight?
- Will the training help remove individual blockages?
- How motivated is Luke to increase his fighting abilities?

Joseph E. Champoux

CONCEPTS OR EXAMPLES

- ☐ Motivation
- ☐ Expectancy theory
- ☐ Effort-performance expectancy
- ☐ Organizational blockages
- ☐ Individual blockages

- ☐ Skills and abilities
- ☐ Training
- ☐ Performance-outcome expectancy
- ☐ Valence

ANALYSIS

_____
_____
_____
_____
_____
_____
_____
_____
_____

PERSONAL REACTIONS

_____
_____
_____
_____
_____
_____
_____
_____
_____

Mr. Holland's Opus

Color, 1995
Running Time: 2 hours, 22 minutes
Rating: PG
Director: Stephen Herek
Distributor: Buena Vista Home Video

Glenn Holland (Richard Dreyfuss) has an undying passion for music but must leave full-time composing to accept a high school music teacher's job. Originally intended as a temporary position, Mr. Holland stays for thirty years. During that time, he discovers his gifts as a teacher and his ability to motivate his students to high performance.

SCENES

DVD CHAPTER 10. NEW ASSIGNMENT TO CHAPTER 11. CHALLENGED (0:43:28–0:53:53)

This sequence starts on the school's football field after Mr. Holland's unsuccessful effort at getting the band to march correctly. It follows Mr. Holland's discussion with Principal Jacobs (Olympia Dukakis) and Vice Principal Wolters (William H. Macy) about the type of music he teaches. They appointed him the head of the marching band.

Observing that Mr. Holland has great difficulty getting the band to march correctly, Coach Meister (Jay Thomas) intervenes. The sequence ends after Mr. Holland and the band congratulate Lou (Terrence Howard) for getting the beat. The film cuts to the town's parade.

WHAT TO WATCH FOR AND ASK YOURSELF

- What motivation method does Mr. Holland use to motivate Lou Russ to learn to play the drum?
- Does he change Lou's playing behavior gradually or in one large change?
- What happens to Lou's self-esteem as these scenes unfold?

CONCEPTS OR EXAMPLES

- ☐ Motivation
- ☐ Behavior modification
- ☐ Shaping
- ☐ Positive reinforcement
- ☐ Self-esteem

ANALYSIS

_____

_____

_____

_____

_____

_____

_____

_____

_____

_____

PERSONAL REACTIONS

_____

_____

_____

_____

_____

_____

_____

_____

_____

CHAPTER 14
Job Design and Intrinsic Rewards

Organizations and managers create a context within which employees can experience **intrinsic rewards**, rewards that people give to themselves. Although managers can use extrinsic or external rewards directly, they have only indirect control over intrinsic rewards. A manager cannot tell an employee to experience intrinsic rewards such as self-esteem or self-actualization. The manager can only create job experiences that let employees experience those rewards.

Job design and **job redesign** help managers create intrinsically motivating work. The primary method of designing jobs well into the 20th century used task specialization. People did small tasks repeatedly. Although workers could do such jobs more efficiently, there were many human costs. Jobs that had small, repeated tasks created boredom and dissatisfaction among those doing the jobs.[80] By the early 1940s, different work redesign methods emerged to reduce task specialization's negative effects.[81]

Job rotation moved the same worker among different jobs. **Job enlargement** added duties and tasks to a job. **Job enrichment** also repackaged duties, but increased worker autonomy and responsibility.[82]

The following films show aspects of job design and intrinsic rewards:

- *Tower Heist*
- *Joe Versus the Volcano*
- *Modern Times*
- *Morning Glory*

---

[80] Harold L. Sheppard and Neal Q. Herrick, *Where Have All the Robots Gone? Worker Dissatisfaction in the '70s* (New York: Free Press, 1972); Charles R. Walker and Robert Guest, *The Man on the Assembly Line* (Cambridge, MA: Harvard University Press, 1952).

[81] Ricky W. Griffin, *Task Design: An Integrative Approach* (Glenview, IL: Scott, Foresman, 1982); J. Richard Hackman, "Work Design," in *Improving Life at Work: Behavioral Science Approaches to Organizational Change*, ed. J. Richard Hackman and J. Lloyd Suttle (Santa Monica, CA: Goodyear Publishing Company, Inc., 1977), chap. 3; J. Richard Hackman and Greg R. Oldham, *Work Redesign* (Reading, MA: Addison-Wesley, 1980); Greg R. Oldham, "Job Design," in *International Review of Industrial and Organizational Psychology*, ed. Cary L. Cooper and Ivan T. Robertson (Chichester, England: John Wiley & Sons, Ltd., 1996), chap. 2.

[82] Frederick Herzberg, "One More Time: How Do You Motivate Employees?" *Harvard Business Review* 46 (January-February, 1968): 53–62.

Joseph E. Champoux

Tower Heist shows the condominium's manager and several staff trying to steal $20 million from the hotel's owner. *Joe Versus the Volcano* has scenes that emphasize a negative work context's effect on people's responses to their job's intrinsic qualities. *Modern Times* offers a satirical look through the eyes of Charlie Chaplin's Little Tramp character at 1930s manufacturing jobs. *Morning Glory* focuses on a young executive producer charged with turning around a low rated news show.

Tower Heist

Color, 2011
Running Time: 1 hour, 44 minutes
Rating: PG-13
Director: Brett Ratner
Distributor: Universal Studios Home Entertainment.

Employees of The Tower, an exclusive and expensive condominium complex, have lost their pensions to Arthur Shaw (Alan Alda), the owner of the building. Convinced that the $20 million is hidden in Shaw's penthouse, Josh Kovaks (Ben Stiller) the building manager enlists the aid of several of his employees. Especially important for safe cracking is the unexpected staffer Odessa (Gabourey Sidibe). Slide (Eddie Murphy), a petty crook, adds to the excitement.

SCENES

DVD CHAPTER 2 (0:03:23–0:08:08)

These scenes begin as Lester (Stephen Henderson) and the other doorman (Steven Weisz) open the door for Arthur Shaw. Lester says, "Good morning Mr. Shaw. You are looking lean and mean today." The scenes end after Enrique Dev'Reaux (Michael Peña) asks about tips and Josh says, "We don't. We never take tips at The Tower." Charlie (Casey Affleck) arrives and Josh begins to talk to him.

WHAT TO WATCH FOR AND ASK YOURSELF

- Rate the core job characteristics of Josh Kovaks' job. Use a 1 to 7 scale where 1 is low on a job characteristic and 7 is high on a job characteristic.
- Rate the work context satisfaction (supervision, coworkers, physical environment) of his job. Use a 1 to 7 scale where 1 is low satisfaction and 7 is high satisfaction.
- Do intrinsic and extrinsic rewards play a role in these scenes?

CONCEPTS OR EXAMPLES

- ☐ Job design
- ☐ Technical process and job design
- ☐ Intrinsic motivation
- ☐ Work context satisfaction
- ☐ Core job characteristics
- ☐ No extrinsic rewards

ANALYSIS

_____

_____

_____

_____

_____

_____

_____

_____

_____

PERSONAL REACTIONS

_____

_____

_____

_____

_____

_____

_____

_____

_____

Joe Versus the Volcano (II)

Color, 1990
Running Time: 1 hour, 42 minutes
Rating: PG
Director: John Patrick Shanley
Distributor: Warner Home Video

"**O**nce upon a time there was a guy named Joe who had a very lousy job..." This film's opening title screens give strong clues about a typical workday for Joe Banks (Tom Hanks). He has a bad job and perhaps an even worse work environment. Joe does not feel well. Joe learns from his doctor that he has a "brain cloud," a rare disease that will kill him in less than six months. He accepts millionaire Samuel Harvey Graynamore's (Lloyd Bridges) offer of a vacation on Waponi Woo, a South Sea Island where he will live like a king. The bad part of the vacation comes when he learns he must jump into a local volcano as part of an island ritual.

Note: Chapter 8 "Attitudes" also discusses scenes from this film.

SCENES

DVD CHAPTER 2 WHAT'S THE MATTER? (0:05:08–0:11:19)

These scenes start as Joe Banks hangs his hat and coat on the coat rack after entering the office. The scenes end after Joe puts his hands to his face and you hear the voice-over, "Mr. Banks." The film cuts to Dr. Ellison's (Robert Stack) office where Joe learns he has a brain cloud.

WHAT TO WATCH FOR AND ASK YOURSELF

- What features of Joe's work context (supervision, coworkers, physical environment) affect his job reactions?
- Do those features have positive or negative effects?
- Rate Joe's satisfaction with his work context. Use a 1 to 7 scale where 1 is low satisfaction and 7 is high satisfaction.

CONCEPTS OR EXAMPLES

- [ ] Physical work environment
- [ ] Work context effects on reactions to job characteristics
- [ ] Work context
- [ ] Coworkers
- [ ] Supervisory behavior
- [ ] Work context satisfaction

ANALYSIS

_____

_____

_____

_____

_____

_____

_____

_____

_____

PERSONAL REACTIONS

_____

_____

_____

_____

_____

_____

_____

_____

_____

_____

Modern Times

Black and White, 1936
Running Time: 1 hour, 23 minutes
Rating: G
Director: Charlie Chaplin
Distributor: Warner Home Video

Charlie Chaplin produced and directed this film and wrote its script and music. It is his last silent film and his first with sound.[83] It is an engaging satirical portrayal of factory work of the period. The feeding machine sequence early in the film is one of many comic highlights that one should not miss. *Modern Times* ranks among the top 100 films of the American Film Institute and the Library of Congress' National Film Registry.[84]

Chaplin plays a factory worker who tightens bolts on nondescript parts that flow endlessly by him. He cracks under the stress of this work and runs crazily through the factory. The entire film features Chaplin trying to rebuild his life around his wife, the lovely Paulette Goddard. They eventually give up in the city and search for a better life elsewhere.

SCENES

DVD CHAPTER 01 TO CHAPTER 02 (0:00:54–0:05:11)

These scenes start after the opening credits with a text screen, "Modern Times. A story of industry, of individual enterprise ~ humanity crusading in the pursuit of happiness." They end as Chaplin takes his break and lights a cigarette in the bathroom. The Electro Steel Corp. president (Al Ernest Garcia) comes on the bathroom video screen and yells, "Hey!" to Chaplin.

WHAT TO WATCH FOR AND ASK YOURSELF

- Predict a motivating potential score (MPS) for these jobs. On a seven-point scale, MPS can range from a low of 1 to a high of 343.
- How do you rate the work context (supervision, coworkers, physical environment)? Use a 1 to 7 scale where 1 is poor and 7 is great.
- Does the job characteristics theory of work motivation predict the behavior shown in the scenes?

---

[83] Maltin, *Leonard Maltin's Movie Guide*, 941; Geoffrey Nowell-Smith, ed., *The Oxford History of World Cinema* (Oxford: Oxford University Press, 1996), 84–85.

[84] Craddock, *VideoHound's Golden Movie Retriever*, 694.

CONCEPTS OR EXAMPLES

☐ Job design
☐ Assembly line technology
☐ Serial interdependence
☐ Work context
☐ Supervisory behavior

☐ Coworkers
☐ Job characteristics theory of work motivation
☐ Motivating potential score
☐ Growth satisfaction

ANALYSIS

_____

_____

_____

_____

_____

_____

_____

_____

_____

PERSONAL REACTIONS

_____

_____

_____

_____

_____

_____

_____

_____

_____

Morning Glory

Color, 2010
Running Time: 1 hour, 47 minutes
Rating: PG-13
Director: Roger Michell
Distributor: Paramount Home Entertainment

Becky Fuller (Rachel McAdams) takes on the challenge of reinvigorating a failing news show as its new executive producer. Complications to her effort come from grouchy news anchor Mike Pomeroy (Harrison Ford) and diva news anchor Colleen Peck (Diane Keaton). Becky tries to get them to cooperate fully, at least during a newscast.

SCENES

DVD CHAPTER 4 (0:19:22–0:22:10)

These scenes start as Becky Fuller and Lenny Bergman (John Pankow) enter the meeting room. Becky says, "Hi. Hi everyone. I'm Becky." She proceeds with a high speed meeting. At the end of the meeting she fires news anchor Paul McVee (Ty Burrell). She receives applause for her action.

WHAT TO WATCH FOR AND ASK YOURSELF

- Does Becky Fuller's job have low, middle, or high motivating potential?
- What levels of intrinsic motivation, growth satisfaction, and job satisfaction do you perceive for Becky? Low, middle, or high?
- Could such a job exist in the real world?

CONCEPTS OR EXAMPLES

- ☐ Work environment
- ☐ Growth satisfaction
- ☐ General satisfaction
- ☐ Job dissatisfaction
- ☐ Internal work motivation
- ☐ Motivation potential

ANALYSIS

_____

_____

_____

_____

_____

_____

_____

_____

_____

_____

PERSONAL REACTIONS

_____

_____

_____

_____

_____

_____

_____

_____

_____

_____

CHAPTER 15
Groups and Intergroup Processes

Groups can powerfully affect people's behavior. Knowledge of how and why groups form, and an understanding of their dynamics, can help you function better within a group or manage group activities.[85]

A **group** is a collection of people trying to do a task or reach a goal. The people regularly interact with each other and depend on each other to do their tasks. The degree of mutual dependence is a function of people's job design and the organization's design.

Formal groups are either functional groups within an organization or task groups.[86] Functional groups are clusters of people formed by the organization's design into departments and work units. Such groups are often permanent, but may change if the organization redesigns its structure.

Interaction patterns within organizations can affect the formation of informal groups within and across formal groups. **Informal groups** may form along interest lines, such as people's task specialization, hobbies, or other interests. Such groups form a "shadow organization" applying powerful forces, both good and bad, on the formal organization.[87]

The scenes described in this chapter show groups and intergroup processes in action. Scenes included here come from:

- *The Dirty Dozen*
- *Hoosiers*
- *Le Mans*
- *Mr. Mom*

The Dirty Dozen shows a cohesive group in action. *Hoosiers* offers contrasting scenes about groups, group dynamics, and intergroup processes. The *Le Mans* pit stop sequence shows a group's performance while doing interdependent tasks. The scenes from *Mr. Mom* show various stages of group development.

---

[85] John M. Levine and Richard L. Moreland, "Progress in Small Group Research," in *Annual Review of Psychology*, vol. 41, ed. Mark R. Rosensweig and Lyman W. Porter (Palo Alto, CA: Annual Reviews Inc., 1990), 585–634.

[86] Dorwin Cartwright and Alvin Frederick Zander, *Group Dynamics: Research and Theory* (New York: Harper & Row, Publishers, Inc., 1968), 36–38; A. Paul Hare, *Groups, Teams, and Social Interaction: Theories and Applications* (New York: Praeger, 1992).

[87] Robert F. Allen and Saul Pilnick, "Confronting the Shadow Organization: How to Detect and Defeat Negative Norms," *Organizational Dynamics* 1, no. 4 (1973): 6–10.

The Dirty Dozen (I)

Color, 1967
Running Time: 2 hours, 30 minutes
Rating: NR
Director: Robert Aldrich
Distributor: Warner Home Video

Army Major Reisman (Lee Marvin) has the almost impossible task of developing a team of twelve men for action behind the lines against the Germans in World War II. He recruits his men from the murderers, thieves, and rapists in an army prison and makes a deal with them: successfully complete the mission and the Army will commute their sentences. The mission: parachute behind enemy lines at night and blow up a chateau full of German officers before D-Day.

Note: Chapter 23 "Organizational Design" also discusses scenes from this film.

SCENES

DVD CHAPTER 19 BREED CONTEMPT (1:14:04–1:20:46)

The scenes start as a jeep pulls up to the gate of the Dirty Dozen's compound and Corporal Morgan (Robert Phillips) says, "This is a restricted area, Sir." They follow the graduation celebration with drinking and dancing. The scenes end after Colonel Breed (Robert Ryan) and his troops leave the compound. The film cuts to a shot of Major General Worden (Ernest Borgnine) and a heated discussion about the behavior of Major Reisman's men.

WHAT TO WATCH FOR AND ASK YOURSELF

- Is the Dirty Dozen a cohesive group? Why or why not?
- What function does this group serve for its members?
- Is their behavior dysfunctional for their organization, the U.S. Army?

CONCEPTS OR EXAMPLES

☐ Groups
☐ Cohesiveness
☐ Norms

☐ Conformity to group norms
☐ Functions of groups
☐ Superordinate goal

ANALYSIS

_____
_____
_____
_____
_____
_____
_____
_____
_____
_____

PERSONAL REACTIONS

_____
_____
_____
_____
_____
_____
_____
_____
_____
_____

Hoosiers

Color, 1987
Running Time: 1 hour, 54 minutes
Rating: PG
Director: David Anspaugh
Distributor: MGM/UA Home Entertainment

New high school basketball coach Norman Dale (Gene Hackman) transforms a losing team into a tournament-winning team. He is a former college coach who was forced out of coaching eleven years earlier. The setting is 1950s basketball-loving Indiana. This film chronicles the transformation of a small-town team unaccustomed to change into one with a succession of wins.

SCENES

DVD CHAPTER 4. WARM WELCOME THROUGH CHAPTER 5. FIRST PRACTICE (0:08:49–0:18:55)

These scenes follow Coach Dale moving into his apartment on Principal Cletus Summer's (Sheb Wooley) farm. They begin with Dale meeting some townspeople in the barbershop. The scenes open with George (Chelcie Ross) saying, "The last time you coached was 12 years ago?" George is the Assistant Coach of the Hickory High School basketball team. They end after the practice session in the gym. The film cuts to a street scene and a café with Dale and Principal Summer drinking coffee.

WHAT TO WATCH FOR AND ASK YOURSELF

- What factors contribute to the team's lack of cohesiveness before Coach Dale arrives?
- How does Dale transform the team to a cohesive, winning team?
- What are this group's norms?

CONCEPTS OR EXAMPLES

☐ Group dynamics

☐ Cohesiveness

☐ Norms

☐ Non-cohesive group

☐ Cohesive group formation

☐ High-performance team

☐ Factors affecting cohesive group formation

ANALYSIS

_____

_____

_____

_____

_____

_____

_____

_____

_____

PERSONAL REACTIONS

_____

_____

_____

_____

_____

_____

_____

_____

_____

_____

Le Mans

Color, 1971
Running Time: 1 hour, 46 minutes
Rating: G
Director: Lee H. Katzin
Distributor: Paramount Home Video

This Steve McQueen film features dramatic real footage of the legendary Le Mans 24-hour Grand Prix endurance race. Top race driver Michael Delaney (Steve McQueen) avoids emotional involvement and competes relentlessly to win. The tension builds when he crashes his car and drops out of the race. Team manager David Townsend (Ronald Leigh-Hunt) asks Michael if he feels well enough to reenter the race in its final eight minutes. Townsend wants the Gulf-Porsche team to win. The team's pit crew works in a high-pressure, interdependent environment. Documentary style cinematography gives exciting racing scenes for a film with a minimal plot. McQueen did his own driving in this film.

SCENES

There are two sets of scenes that appear early and late in the film. The first set shows the pit crew in action on the Gulf-Porsche team car. The second set shows the result of the team's efforts.

DVD CHAPTER 6. COMPETING FOR FIRST PLACE (0:49:38–0:52:49)

These scenes start with the sound of a siren and a close-up of a loudspeaker announcing two car accidents including a Gulf-Porsche team car. The accidents occurred just before these scenes at Indianapolis Corner. Team manager Townsend says, "Bring them in for rain tires." Michael's car is the only one left for the Gulf-Porsche team. These scenes end with Townsend's assistant checking a stopwatch and Townsend watching the car leave the pit. The film cuts to another Shell team Ferrari arriving in the pits.

DVD CHAPTER 12. THE WINNER! (1:40:49–1:43:47)

The second set of scenes shows the race's end. It starts with a shot of a checkered flag. The scenes end after David Townsend thanks Michael.

WHAT TO WATCH FOR AND ASK YOURSELF

- Does this type of work require a team approach or could a single person do it?
- Is this a cohesive group? If *yes*, what are its likely behavioral norms?
- What helped the Gulf-Porsche team succeed in getting their car out of the pit before the Ferrari team?

CONCEPTS OR EXAMPLES

- ☐ Groups
- ☐ Interdependence
- ☐ Group behavior
- ☐ Norms

- ☐ Self-managing team
- ☐ Cohesiveness
- ☐ Individual versus group performance

ANALYSIS

_____

_____

_____

_____

_____

_____

_____

_____

PERSONAL REACTIONS

_____

_____

_____

_____

_____

_____

_____

_____

_____

Mr. Mom

Color, 1983
Running Time: 1 hour, 31 minutes
Rating: PG
Director: Stan Dragoti
Distributor: MGM Home Entertainment

Jack Butler (Michael Keaton) becomes unemployed after his layoff from his auto executive job. The family still needs money so wife Caroline (Teri Garr) goes back to work. Jack's days are now spent tending to their three children and keeping up with endless housework. A group of female neighbors who enjoy card games and drinking serve as a significant distraction for Jack. His challenges increase with the presence of one neighbor who wants to pursue him and a vacuum cleaner with a mind of its own.

SCENES

DVD CHAPTER 6. THE JUNGLE OUT THERE (0:16:07–0:19:37)

These scenes start with an upward panning shot of a high-rise building. Caroline nervously rides the elevator to her interview appointment at the Richardson/Frankel Advertising firm. These scenes end after her aborted review of some tuna fish advertising recommendations. She says, "When was the last time any of you people were in a supermarket?" The film cuts to Jack pushing a shopping cart in a supermarket.

WHAT TO WATCH FOR AND ASK YOURSELF

- Which stage of group development do these scenes show?
- Do people show behaviors typical for the stage you identified? Give some examples.
- Is this a cohesive or non-cohesive group? What is the evidence for your conclusion?

CONCEPTS OR EXAMPLES

☐ Stages of group development   ☐ Task focus

☐ Group cohesion stage (norming)   ☐ Dysfunctional conflict

☐ Intragroup conflict stage (storming)   ☐ Group formation stage (forming)

                                              ☐ Termination

ANALYSIS

_____

_____

_____

_____

_____

_____

_____

_____

_____

PERSONAL REACTIONS

_____

_____

_____

_____

_____

_____

_____

_____

_____

_____

CHAPTER 16

Conflict in Organizations

Conflict in organizations is opposition, incompatible behavior, or antagonistic interaction.[88] Conflict includes interactions in which one party opposes another party, or one party tries to block another party from reaching his or her goals. Critical elements of conflict are interdependence with another party and the perception of incompatible goals. The parties in conflict can be individuals or entire groups within an organization.[89]

Conflict happens in a series of episodes. As the **conflict episodes** ebb and flow, periods of cooperation may occur.[90]

Conflict in organizations serves useful functions when properly managed. Cooperation is not the only desirable state within an organization. Having cooperation without any conflict could result in a stagnant organization and complacent management.[91]

These films have excellent scenes showing different aspects of conflict and conflict management:

- *Fried Green Tomatoes*
- *Butch Cassidy and the Sundance Kid*
- *The Odd Couple*
- *Zero Dark Thirty*

Fried Green Tomatoes has scenes showing some important parts of a conflict episode. Scenes from *Butch Cassidy and the Sundance Kid* show all aspects of a conflict episode. *The Odd Couple* has some humorous scenes that reveal how two different personalities reduce their conflict. *Zero Dark Thirty* dramatically captures the complex effort to eliminate Osama bin Laden.

---

[88]   Dean Tjosvold, *The Conflict-Positive Organization: Stimulate Diversity and Create Unity* (Reading, MA: Addison-Wesley Longman, 1991), 33.

[89]   L. David Brown, *Managing Conflict at Organizational Interfaces* (Reading, MA: Addison-Wesley, 1983); Dean G. Pruitt and Sung Hee Kim, *Social Conflict: Escalation, Stalemate, and Settlement*, 3rd. ed. (New York: McGraw-Hill, 2003).

[90]   Louis R. Pondy, "Organizational Conflict: Concepts and Models," *Administrative Science Quarterly*, 12, no. 2 (1967): 296–320.

[91]   Steven P. Robbins, *Managing Organizational Conflict* (Englewood Cliffs, NJ: Prentice Hall, 1974), 28; Tjosvold, *Conflict-Positive Organization.*

Fried Green Tomatoes

Color, 1991
Running Time: 2 hours, 10 minutes
Rating: PG-13
Director: Jon Avnet
Distributor: MCA/Universal Home Video

Repressed Southern housewife Evelyn Couch (Kathy Bates) lives in the small southern town of Whistle Stop, Alabama. She meets spry, elderly Ninnie Threadgoode (Jessica Tandy) while visiting her complaining mother-in-law at a nursing home. Ninnie's story of two women who lived fifty years earlier inspires Evelyn to take charge of her life. She develops an alter ego Towanda, a more independent person determined to improve her boring marriage and reclaim her life.

SCENES

DVD CHAPTER 27 TOWANDA THE AVENGER (1:20:59–1:23:06)

These scenes open in the Winn-Dixie grocery store parking lot. They follow the scenes in which Idgie Threadgoode (Mary Stuart Masterson) and Ruth Jamison (Mary-Louise Parker) discuss Frank Bennett's (Nick Searcy) death. These scenes fade in from a shot of Ruth's face to the parking lot. Evelyn Couch looks for a parking space. The scenes end as Evelyn drives away and the film cuts to an outside shot of the nursing home.[92]

WHAT TO WATCH FOR AND ASK YOURSELF

- Does Evelyn expect to enter a conflict episode in the parking lot?
- What is the latent conflict in the episode?
- Describe the manifest conflict? What does Evelyn do to end the conflict episode?

---

[92] Recommended by Laura Dufek, MBA student, The Robert O. Anderson School of Management, The University of New Mexico.

CONCEPTS OR EXAMPLES

☐ Manifest conflict   ☐ Perceived conflict
☐ Latent conflict   ☐ Conflict episode
☐ Felt conflict   ☐ Conflict aftermath
☐ Conflict reduction   ☐ Conflict orientation

ANALYSIS

_____

_____

_____

_____

_____

_____

_____

_____

_____

PERSONAL REACTIONS

_____

_____

_____

_____

_____

_____

_____

_____

_____

_____

Butch Cassidy and the Sundance Kid (I)

Color, 1969
Running Time: 1 hour, 50 minutes
Rating: PG
Director: George Roy Hill
Distributor: 20th Century Fox Home Entertainment

This seriocomic Western takes liberties with the lives of two legendary 1890's bank robbers. It has many memorable scenes, including a bicycle-riding scene that showcases Burt Bacharach's Oscar-winning song, "Raindrops Keep Fallin' On My Head". William Goldman's script is so sharp that you hang onto every line of dialogue. Director George Roy Hill's effort is a study of and a social commentary on the twilight of that American myth known as the Old West. Much happens along the way as a posse chases the pair, who eventually fight a large group of Bolivian police. A clever script and well-developed characters quickly made this film a classic.[93]

Note: Chapter 20 "Decision Making" also discusses scenes from this film.

SCENES

DVD CHAPTER 4 THE HOLE IN THE WALL THROUGH CHAPTER 5 HOW HARVEY SEES IT (0:09:06–0:15:37)

This sequence starts with Butch Cassidy (Paul Newman) and the Sundance Kid (Robert Redford) riding to the gang's hideout in Hole-in-the-Wall, Wyoming. It follows the poker game scene in which a player (Sam Elliott) accused Sundance of cheating. The sequence ends after Butch says, "Well I'll tell you something, fellas. That's exactly what we're gonna do." The film cuts to steam locomotive smoke as The Flyer goes through a canyon.

WHAT TO WATCH FOR AND ASK YOURSELF

- Does Butch Cassidy slowly perceive that a conflict episode begins? When? What is the evidence in these scenes?
- What is the latent conflict that starts this conflict episode?
- What method of conflict reduction does he use? Will it likely end the episode with no conflict aftermath?

---

[93] Craddock, *VideoHound's Golden Movie Retriever*, 187.

CONCEPTS OR EXAMPLES

- ☐ Conflict episode
- ☐ Latent conflict
- ☐ Manifest conflict
- ☐ Perceived conflict
- ☐ Felt conflict
- ☐ Conflict reduction
- ☐ Conflict orientation
- ☐ Conflict aftermath

ANALYSIS

_____

_____

_____

_____

_____

_____

_____

_____

_____

PERSONAL REACTIONS

_____

_____

_____

_____

_____

_____

_____

_____

_____

The Odd Couple (III)

Color, 1968
Running Time: 1 hour, 46 minutes
Rating: G
Director: Gene Saks
Distributor: Paramount Home Video

Divorced sportswriter Oscar Madison (Walter Matthau) lets his about-to-become divorced best friend Felix Ungar (Jack Lemmon) move into his eight room New York City apartment. They are entirely mismatched. Oscar is disorganized and sloppy; Felix is organized and tidy. Many interactions center on the Friday night poker game with their circle of friends. This delightfully funny film traces their interactions as Felix gets closer to his divorce and Oscar yearns to live alone again.

Note: Chapter 9 "Personality" and Chapter 12 "Motivation: Need Theories" also discuss scenes from this film.

SCENES

DVD CHAPTER 12. SEPARATE KEYS TO CHAPTER 13. NOW I'M GOING TO TELL YOU OFF (1:22:26–1:33:31)

These scenes start as Oscar arrives and goes to the elevator. They follow the interactions with Cecily (Monica Evans) and Gwendolyn (Carole Shelley). The scenes end as Oscar chases Felix.

WHAT TO WATCH FOR AND ASK YOURSELF

- What is the basis of the latent conflict?
- What is the manifest conflict behavior?
- What conflict reduction method do they use?

Joseph E. Champoux

CONCEPTS OR EXAMPLES

- ☐ Latent conflict
- ☐ Conflict reduction
- ☐ Avoidance
- ☐ Separation
- ☐ Conflict orientation

- ☐ Manifest conflict
- ☐ Felt conflict
- ☐ Perceived conflict
- ☐ Conflict aftermath
- ☐ Conflict episode

ANALYSIS

_____

_____

_____

_____

_____

_____

_____

_____

_____

_____

PERSONAL REACTIONS

_____

_____

_____

_____

_____

_____

_____

_____

_____

Zero Dark Thirty

Color, 2012
Running Time: 2 hours, 37 minutes
Rating: R
Director: Kathryn Bigelow
Distributor: Sony Pictures Home Entertainment

The goal: find and kill Osama bin Laden. Military operatives and elite intelligence teams worked for many years to reach that goal. Maya (Jessica Chastain) joins the search with extraordinary commitment to finding bin Laden. This film closes with the night time raid on bin Laden's Pakistan residence.

SCENES

DVD CHAPTER 9 (1:13:33–1:20:22)

These scenes begin with a dark screen followed by the word "TRADECRAFT". They continue with panning images of a communication system. The scenes end after the heated conflict interaction between Maya and her boss Joseph Bradley (Kyle Chandler). He enters his meeting room. The film cuts to Maya drinking a beer in a bar. Jack (Harold Perrineau) approaches with her new cellular telephone. These scenes have several instances of R-rated language.

WHAT TO WATCH FOR AND ASK YOURSELF

- When does Maya perceive herself in conflict with Larry (Édgar Ramirez) from Ground Branch?[94] How do they resolve that conflict?
- When do Maya and Joseph Bradley perceive themselves in conflict? Does felt conflict characterize their conflict episode?
- Which conflict reduction method ends the conflict between Maya and Joseph?

---

[94] Maya does not use Larry's name in these scenes.

CONCEPTS OR EXAMPLES

☐ Conflict episodes

☐ Latent conflict

☐ Felt conflict

☐ Manifest conflict

☐ Conflict aftermath

☐ Conflict reduction method(s)

☐ Conflict orientation

ANALYSIS

_____

_____

_____

_____

_____

_____

_____

_____

_____

_____

PERSONAL REACTIONS

_____

_____

_____

_____

_____

_____

_____

_____

_____

_____

_____

CHAPTER 17
Leadership and Management

Leadership is a social influence process involving two or more people: the leader and a follower or a potential follower.[95] The influence process has two dimensions. The first is the leader's intention to affect the behavior of at least one other person. The second is the extent the target perceives the influence as acceptable. Perception and attribution are important elements of the leadership process. The person who is the influence target must attribute the influence to a specific person and perceive it as acceptable.

Leaders can hold formal organization positions or emerge spontaneously within an organization. The formal positions carry titles such as Manager, Supervisor, or Vice-President. Both the position's qualities and the characteristics of the person holding it contribute to leadership. Other people who are not in formally appointed positions can also play leadership roles. Such leaders are **emergent leaders** and are often found within formal and informal groups in organizations.

Managers and leaders differ. **Managers** sustain and control organizations; **leaders** try to change them. Managers follow the present vision for the organization; they do not create a new one. Leaders have a vision of a desired future state of an organization and inspire followers to pursue that vision.

This chapter discusses leadership scenes from the following films:

- *The American President*
- *Lincoln*
- *Norma Rae*
- *Star Trek: Generations*

The American President has early scenes showing different leadership traits of the President and some key staff members. *Lincoln* shows President Lincoln in a strong leadership interaction. *Norma Rae* portrays a woman in a leadership role. The opening scenes of *Star Trek: Generations* effectively show both the absence and presence of leadership.

---

[95] Bernard M. Bass and Ruth Bass, *The Bass Handbook of Leadership: Theory, Research, and Managerial Applications*, 4th ed. (New York: The Free Press, 2008); Robert J. House and Ram N. Aditya, "The Social Scientific Study of Leadership: Quo Vadis?" *Journal of Management* 23, no. 3 (1997), 409–73; Robert J. House and Mary L. Baetz, "Leadership: Some Empirical Generalizations and New Research Directions," in *Research in Organizational Behavior*, vol 1, ed. Barry M. Staw (Greenwich, CT: JAI Press, 1979), 341–423; Paul C. Nutt and Robert W. Backoff, "Crafting Vision," *Journal of Management Inquiry* 6, no. 4 (1997): 308–28.

The American President

Color, 1995
Running Time: 1 hour, 54 minutes
Rating: PG-13
Director: Rob Reiner
Distributor: Warner Home Video

President Andrew Shepherd (Michael Douglas), a widower, decides to romantically pursue lobbyist Sydney Ellen Wade (Annette Benning). He does not realistically assess the political implications of his involvement with Wade, leading him to reassess his commitment to her and the country. The portrayal of the President as witty, handsome, honest, and decisive will both fit and not fit stereotypes of American Presidents. This film ranked 75th in the American Film Institute's 2002 ranking of cinema love stories.[96]

SCENES

DVD CHAPTER 1 PRESIDENTIAL CREDITS. THROUGH CHAPTER 2 MONDAY MORNING. (0:02:36–0:08:01)

These scenes start after the opening credits. They begin with a shot of the White House. Secret Service Agent Cooper (Beau Billingslea) says into his microphone, "Liberty's moving." President Andrew Shepherd enters the hallway in the background with his assistant Janie (Samantha Mathis). The scenes end after President Shepherd leaves the room following his Monday morning staff meeting. He asks Janie what is next on his calendar. The film cuts to a street shot.

WHAT TO WATCH FOR AND ASK YOURSELF

- Which leadership traits does the President show?
- Which leadership traits does Chief of Staff A. J. MacInery (Martin Sheen) show?
- Which leadership traits does Lewis Rothschild (Michael J. Fox) show?

---

[96] Germain, "'Casablanca' Top Romance Film," C13.

CONCEPTS OR EXAMPLES

☐ Leadership   ☐ Intelligence

☐ Leadership traits   ☐ Energy

☐ Dominance   ☐ Task-relevant knowledge

☐ Self-confidence   ☐ Honesty/integrity

ANALYSIS

_____

_____

_____

_____

_____

_____

_____

_____

_____

PERSONAL REACTIONS

_____

_____

_____

_____

_____

_____

_____

_____

_____

_____

Lincoln

Color, 2012
Running Time: 2 hours, 30 minutes
Rating: PG-13
Director: Steven Spielberg
Distributor: Buena Vista Home Entertainment, Inc.

Daniel Day-Lewis gives an Academy Award-winning performance as Abraham Lincoln, the 16th President of the United States. The film focuses on his last four months in office up to the time of his assassination. During this period, Lincoln focused on abolishing slavery and ending the Civil War.

SCENES

DVD CHAPTER 14. FAIRNESS AND FREEDOM (1:43:42–1:46:33)

These scenes open with Preston Blair (Hal Holbrook) saying "We've managed our members to a fare-thee-well." They follow Lincoln's discussion with Mr. Hutton (David Warshofsky). The scenes end after President Lincoln says, "You will procure me these votes." The film cuts to a wide shot of the House of Representatives chamber. Titling on the screen reads, "THE MORNING OF THE VOTE. JANUARY 31, 1865." Thadeus Stevens (Tommy Lee Jones) enters the chamber from the left.

WHAT TO WATCH FOR AND ASK YOURSELF

- Does President Lincoln have a vision for the United States?
- Does he express himself as a leader: transformational or charismatic?
- Do his cabinet members perceive him as a leader?

CONCEPTS OR EXAMPLES

- ☐ Vision
- ☐ Leadership
- ☐ Values

- ☐ Transformational leadership
- ☐ Charismatic leadership
- ☐ Leadership perceptions

ANALYSIS

_____

_____

_____

_____

_____

_____

_____

_____

_____

_____

PERSONAL REACTIONS

_____

_____

_____

_____

_____

_____

_____

_____

_____

_____

Norma Rae

Color, 1979
Running Time: 1 hour, 57 minutes
Rating: PG
Director: Martin Ritt
Distributor: 20th Century Fox Home Entertainment

This powerful drama shows the struggle of Southern textile workers in forming their first labor union. Reuben (Ron Leibman), a New York City labor organizer, inspires Norma Rae (Sally Field) to organize her fellow workers. Based on true events, Norma Rae's leadership skills get the desired results. Field received a Best Actress Academy Award for her performance.

SCENES

DVD CHAPTER 26. A WOMAN ALONE (1:28:34–1:35:29)

These scenes follow Norma Rae's earlier unsuccessful effort to copy a memo posted by plant management. The memo claimed Black workers would try to dominate the union and the White workers. The scenes begin with a shot of a door and the sign, "Transfer Traffic Only." Norma Rae opens the door and goes to the bulletin board to copy the memo. They end after Mr. Mason (Noble Willingham), the plant manager, enters his office and closes the door. The film cuts to an outside shot of a police car.

WHAT TO WATCH FOR AND ASK YOURSELF

- Which leadership traits does Norma Rae have?
- Do the workers begin to perceive her as a leader?
- Which views (theories) of leadership does she portray?

CONCEPTS OR EXAMPLES

- ☐ Charisma
- ☐ Leadership behavior
- ☐ Leadership mystique
- ☐ Self-confidence
- ☐ Energy
- ☐ Transformational leadership

ANALYSIS

_____

_____

_____

_____

_____

_____

_____

_____

_____

_____

_____

PERSONAL REACTIONS

_____

_____

_____

_____

_____

_____

_____

_____

_____

_____

_____

Star Trek: Generations

Color, 1994
Running Time: 1 hour, 51 minutes
Rating: PG
Director: David Carson
Distributor: Paramount Home Video

Retired Captain James T. Kirk (William Shatner) and fellow retired Starfleet officers, engineer Scotty (James Doohan) and Russian navigator Chekov (Walter Koenig), are guests aboard the Enterprise-B. The first flight of this newly christened starship presents several crises and decisions to people in leadership roles. The film later features Captain Jean-Luc Picard (Patrick Stewart) in an action-filled adventure that shows different people's leadership characteristics in various situations.

SCENES

DVD CHAPTER 01 LIVING LEGENDS TO CHAPTER 02 DISTRESS CALL (0:02:58–0:11:52)

These scenes start at the end of the opening credits with a shot of the Enterprise-B docked in a spaceport. The text on the screen reads, "Directed by David Carson." These scenes end after Scotty transports the second El Aurian ship's survivors to the Enterprise-B. He sadly says to Captain Kirk, "I got forty-seven out of 150." The film cuts to the starship rocking from another blast.

WHAT TO WATCH FOR AND ASK YOURSELF

- What leadership traits do you ascribe to Captain Harriman (Alan Ruck)?
- What leadership traits do you ascribe to Captain Kirk?
- Which leadership theories best describe the behavior of the two captains?

CONCEPTS OR EXAMPLES

☐ Leadership
☐ Leadership traits
☐ Transformational leadership
☐ Self-confidence
☐ Intelligence

☐ Charismatic leadership
☐ Leadership mystique
☐ Absence of leadership
☐ Energy
☐ Task-relevant knowledge

ANALYSIS

_____

_____

_____

_____

_____

_____

_____

_____

_____

PERSONAL REACTIONS

_____

_____

_____

_____

_____

_____

_____

_____

_____

_____

CHAPTER 18
Communication

Organizational communication includes the purpose, flow, and direction of messages and the media used for them. Such communication happens within the complex, interdependent social systems of organizations. Think of communication as another view of behavior in organizations, which includes sending, receiving, and giving meaning to messages.[97]

Communication processes in organizations are continuous and constantly changing. They do not have a beginning or an end, nor do they follow a strict sequence. During communication, the sender creates messages from one or more symbols to which the sender attaches meaning. Messages have oral, written, or nonverbal forms. They can also be intentional or unintentional.

Organizational communication happens over a pathway called a **network**, a series of interconnected positions in an organization. The network can be formal as defined by organizational positions and relationships among them. It can also be informal as defined by informal patterns of social interaction. Communication over the network goes in any direction: downward, upward, or horizontal.[98] **Noise** negatively affects communication accuracy by introducing distortions, errors, and foreign matter. The sender does not intend such signal distortions and errors.

Scenes from the following films show different aspects of communication:

- *Milk Money*
- *My Cousin Vinnie*
- ¡Three Amigos!
- *The Naughty Nineties*

Scenes from *Milk Money* and *My Cousin Vinnie* show how different frames of reference affect communication accuracy. The "plethora" scenes from ¡Three Amigos! quickly note how large words do not communicate well. Abbott and Costello's *The Naughty Nineties* has the classic "Who's on First?" skit, which has no parallel for showing communication misunderstandings.

---

[97] Gerald M. Goldhaber, *Organizational Communication*, 4th ed. (Dubuque, IA: Wm. C. Brown, 1986); Mark L. Knapp, Judith A. Hall, and Terrence G. Horgan, *Nonverbal Communication in Human Interaction*, 8th ed. (Boston: Wadsworth, Cengage Learning, 2014); Lyman W. Porter and Karlene H. Roberts, "Communication in Organizations," in *Handbook of Industrial and Organizational Psychology,* ed. Marvin D. Dunnette (Chicago: Rand McNally College Pub. Co., 1976), chap. 35.

[98] Claude Elwood Shannon, Warren Weaver, Richard E. Blahut, and Bruce Hajek, *The Mathematical Theory of Communication* (Urbana, IL: University of Illinois Press, 1998).

Milk Money

Color, 1994
Running Time: 1 hour, 50 minutes
Rating: PG-13
Director: Richard Benjamin
Distributor: *Paramount Home Video*

Three young boys with high sexual curiosity sell their possessions to get enough money to go to the city. They search for a woman who will show them her nude body. After several false starts, and having their bicycles stolen, they meet V (Melanie Griffith), a prostitute. She returns them to their suburban home using her pimp's car, which, unknown to her, has his hidden money. The car breaks down in front of young Frank Wheeler's (Michael Patrick Carter) house. His widower father, Tom Wheeler (Ed Harris), tries to repair the car.

SCENES

DVD CHAPTER 5. THE MATH TUTOR (0:28:41–0:32:44)

These scenes follow V driving Frank and his friends from the big city to their suburban homes. V tries to leave after dropping off Frank but her car does not start. The scenes begin as Frank greets his father at the front door. He introduces V to his father as Brad's (Adam La Vorgna) new math tutor. These scenes end after Tom's futile effort to start V's car. He tells V that Frank is his major concern and "It" is not important to him anymore. V laughs and says "Poor man" as she kisses his cheek. V walks away. Tom looks bewildered while holding the jumper cables. The film cuts to V crossing a street.

WHAT TO WATCH FOR AND ASK YOURSELF

- What is the basis of the misperception shown in these scenes?
- What effect does that misperception have on the communication process?
- Is there any nonverbal communication that should help Tom Wheeler better understand the situation?

CONCEPTS OR EXAMPLES

- ☐ Basic communication process
- ☐ Miscommunication
- ☐ Noise
- ☐ Verbal communication

- ☐ Nonverbal communication
- ☐ Frame of reference
- ☐ Misperception
- ☐ Effective communication

ANALYSIS

_____

_____

_____

_____

_____

_____

_____

_____

_____

PERSONAL REACTIONS

_____

_____

_____

_____

_____

_____

_____

_____

_____

My Cousin Vinnie

Color, 1992
Running Time: 2 hours
Rating: R
Director: Jonathan Lynn
Distributor: 20th Century Fox Home Entertainment

Former Brooklyn automobile mechanic Vincent La Guardia Gambino (Joe Pesci) gets his first case after passing his bar examination, six years after his law school graduation. His cousin Bill Gambino (Ralph Macchio) retains him as his defense attorney in his trial for allegedly murdering a convenience store clerk. Vincent Gambino has no court experience because he passed the bar examination only six weeks ago. His courtroom demeanor reflects his Brooklyn streetwise behavior, putting him into almost constant conflict with conservative judge Chamberlain Haller (Fred Gwynne).

SCENES

DVD EXH. 1 MAIN TITLES: TUNA THIEVES TO EXH. 2 A CONFESSION (0:02:57–0:10:04)

These scenes start as Bill Gambino and Stan Rothenstein (Mitchell Whitfield) drive up to the Sac-O-Suds convenience store in Beechum County, Alabama. They are on their way to UCLA. The scenes appear at the film's beginning toward the end of the opening credits. These scenes end after the overhead shot of Bill and Stan sitting on a bench in handcuffs. They discuss their confusing situation. The film cuts to a sheriff's deputy opening the door and telling them it is time to make their telephone calls. These scenes have some R-rated language.[99]

WHAT TO WATCH FOR AND ASK YOURSELF

- What is the basis of the miscommunication shown in these scenes?
- Are Sheriff Farley (Bruce McGill), Bill, and Stan using the same frame of reference?
- Do these scenes show the cost of miscommunication?

---

[99] Brendan Young, undergraduate student, The Robert O. Anderson School of Management, The University of New Mexico, recommended these scenes.

Joseph E. Champoux

CONCEPTS OR EXAMPLES

- ☐ Miscommunication
- ☐ Noise
- ☐ Effective communication
- ☐ Frame of reference
- ☐ Basic communication process
- ☐ Ineffective communication

ANALYSIS

_____

_____

_____

_____

_____

_____

_____

_____

_____

PERSONAL REACTIONS

_____

_____

_____

_____

_____

_____

_____

_____

_____

¡Three Amigos!

Color, 1986
Running Time: 1 hour, 45 minutes
Rating: PG
Director: John Landis
Distributor: Home Box Office Home Video

A silent film comedy team, The Three Amigos, have a falling out with their studio. They receive a telegram from a desperate citizen of a small Mexican village asking their help in fighting a gang of bandits. The Three Amigos interpret the message as an invitation to perform for 100,000 pesos. A comedy of errors unfolds when they discover there is no performance and the bandits use real bullets.

SCENES

DVD CHAPTER 15. EL GUAPO & THE GERMAN (1:03:05–1:04:13)

These scenes start as El Guapo (Alfonso Arau) rides into the village and says to Jefe (Tony Plana), "Jefe, the German arrive yet?" The scenes follow the preparations for El Guapo's birthday party. They end with El Guapo grinning at Jefe after their short exchange. Their conversation continues with Jefe noting some reasons for El Guapo's behavior.

WHAT TO WATCH FOR AND ASK YOURSELF

- Does Jefe quickly understand El Guapo's meaning of "plethora"? Why?
- Is this effective or ineffective communication? Why?
- How could El Guapo improve his communication effectiveness?

CONCEPTS OR EXAMPLES

- ☐ Noise
- ☐ Miscommunication
- ☐ Effective communication
- ☐ Ineffective communication
- ☐ Functional communication
- ☐ Dysfunctional communication
- ☐ Improving communication effectiveness

ANALYSIS

_____

_____

_____

_____

_____

_____

_____

_____

_____

PERSONAL REACTIONS

_____

_____

_____

_____

_____

_____

_____

_____

_____

_____

The Naughty Nineties

Black and White, 1945
Running Time: 1 hour, 16 minutes
Rating: NR
Director: Jean Yarbrough
Distributor: Universal Studios

Typical Abbott and Costello slapstick humor and verbal banter highlight this film. It focuses on the River Queen, a Mississippi River paddle wheel boat besieged by crooks. A major feature of this otherwise ordinary comedy is the first on-screen presentation of the duo's classic skit, "Who's on First?"[100]. The videocassette box for the Universal Studios Comedy Legends release (2000) of this film says, "Director Jean Yarbrough had such a problem keeping the crew quiet while filming Lou and Bud's famous routine 'Who's on First?' that if you listen closely — you can hear the cameramen and grips laughing in the background!"

SCENES

DVD CHAPTER 12 "WHO'S ON FIRST" (0:39:04–0:45:18)

The "Who's on First" scenes start as Dexter Broadhurst (Bud Abbott) comes on stage with a baseball bat singing, "Take Me Out to the Ball Game." Sebastian Dinwiddle (Lou Costello) comes on stage selling peanuts, popcorn, and Cracker Jacks®. These scenes follow the collage of gambling scenes and the on deck discussion about gambling honesty between Caroline Jackson (Lois Collier) and dishonest gambler Mr. Crawford (Alan Curtis). The skit ends after Sebastian throws down his bat and leers at Dexter. The film cuts to the River Queen's gambling hall. Test your listening skills by trying to identify each player's name and position.

WHAT TO WATCH FOR AND ASK YOURSELF

- Is this an example of functional or dysfunctional communication?
- Does either person listen to what the other says?
- Would active listening have helped their communication?

---

[100] Craddock, *VideoHound's Golden Movie Retriever,* 724

CONCEPTS OR EXAMPLES

- ☐ Functional communication
- ☐ Dysfunctional communication
- ☐ Listening
- ☐ Active listening
- ☐ Noise

ANALYSIS

_____
_____
_____
_____
_____
_____
_____
_____
_____

PERSONAL REACTIONS

_____
_____
_____
_____
_____
_____
_____
_____
_____
_____

CHAPTER 19

Problem Solving

Problems occur in organizations when a situation does not match a desired state.[101] Examples of common organizational problems include major market shifts, over and understaffing, inventory shortages, and customer complaints. Managers can also frame problems as opportunities. A series of customer complaints that focus on common issues, for example, can present managers with opportunities for process improvement.

Problem-solving processes in organizations focus on identifying a problem and finding its root causes. Along with decision-making processes, they are a complex set of processes used by both managers and nonmanagers. The problem-solving process creates options or alternatives that enter a decision-making process (see Chapter 20, "Decision Making"). Managers use the latter process to choose among the options.

Several films offer effective scenes showing problem solving. This chapter discusses scenes from the following films:

- *Apollo 13*
- *The Rock*
- *James and the Giant Peach*
- *Papillon*

Apollo 13 focuses on problem solving, the problem of the astronauts' safe return to earth in their damaged space capsule. *The Rock* has powerful scenes of problem solving involving a lethal gas. *James and the Giant Peach* has some beautifully animated scenes showing complex aspects of problem solving and its links to decision making. The closing scenes of *Papillon* dramatically show how Papillon solves his problem—escape from Devil's Island.

---

[101] Marjorie A. Lyles and Ian I. Mitroff, "Organizational Problem Formulation: An Empirical Study," *Administrative Science Quarterly* 25, no. 1 (1980): 102–19; W. E Pounds, "The Process of Problem Finding," *Industrial Management Review* 11, no. 1 (1969): 1–19.

Apollo 13 (I)

Color, 1995
Running Time: 2 hours, 20 minutes
Rating: PG
Director: Ron Howard
Distributor: Universal Studios Home Video

This film shows the flight of Apollo 13, a NASA mission to the moon that almost ended in disaster. Innovative problem solving and decision making amid massive ambiguity saved the crew. Almost any scene dramatically makes this point. Flight Director Gene Kranz wrote a book describing the mission and the activities that prevented a disaster.[102] The zero gravity simulator, a KC-135 four-engine jet aircraft (NASA's "Vomit Comet"), helped create the film's realistic weightless scenes. These scenes required 600 parabolic loops over 10 days of filming.[103]

Note: Chapter 20 "Decision Making" also discusses scenes from this film.

SCENES

There are two scenes at different points in the film. The first shows the engineers working on the problem. The second shows the astronauts working on the problem.

DVD CHAPTER 35 THE CO2 PROBLEM (1:19:54–1:20:59)

These scenes follow the nearly complete shutdown of Apollo 13. They appear after the short scene of astronauts sleeping on the floor and people discussing the physical condition of the Apollo 13 crew. The scenes start with a wide shot of the Earth-Moon Transit control board in Mission Control. Three men enter and go to flight director Gene Kranz (Ed Harris). One says, "Gene, we have a situation brewing with the carbon dioxide." It ends after the engineers start organizing the material to build the filter. The film cuts to a television set showing old news coverage of the Apollo 13 astronauts.

DVD CHAPTER 39 WITH EVERY BREATH . . . (1:28:01–1:32:53)

These scenes start with a technician (Walter von Huene) carrying a newly built CO2 filter to mission control. They follow the conflict among the Apollo 13 astronauts and the assessment of their CO2 levels. The scenes end after a controller says, "That is good to hear Aquarius." He turns to the engineer and says, "And you Sir are a steely-eyed missile man." The film cuts to astronaut Ken Mattingly (Gary Sinise) in a simulator.

---

[102] Gene Kranz, *Failure Is Not an Option: Mission Control from Mercury to Apollo 13 and Beyond.* (New York: Simon & Shuster, 2000).

[103] Craddock, *VideoHound's Golden Movie Retriever,* 86

WHAT TO WATCH FOR AND ASK YOURSELF

- What is the problem in these scenes?
- What are the engineers' options for solving the problem?
- Are the astronauts problem solving or deciding a course of action?

CONCEPTS OR EXAMPLES

☐ Problem solving   ☐ Decision making

☐ Problem identification   ☐ Innovation

☐ Options, alternatives

ANALYSIS

_____

_____

_____

_____

_____

_____

_____

_____

_____

PERSONAL REACTIONS

_____

_____

_____

_____

_____

_____

_____

_____

_____

The Rock

Color, 1996
Running Time: 2 hours, 16 minutes
Rating: R
Director: Michael Bay
Distributor: Hollywood Pictures Home Video

Disgruntled, decorated Marine Brigadier General Francis X. Hummel (Ed Harris) takes over Alcatraz. He threatens to fire rockets with a deadly gas into San Francisco, in his effort to get benefits for families of slain covert operations soldiers. Previously imprisoned British agent John Patrick Mason (Sean Connery), the only person to escape from Alcatraz, teams with FBI biochemist Dr. Stanley Goodspeed (Nicolas Cage) to lead a team into the prison. Almost continuous action heightens the suspense as the film takes many twists and turns to its conclusion.

SCENES

DVD CHAPTER 2. TAKING OVER TO CHAPTER 3. DANGER ALARM (0:07:57–0:13:07)

These scenes begin with an aerial shot of the FBI Laboratory, Washington, DC. They follow Hummel's rocket stealing operation. The scenes end after Goodspeed tells Carla (Vanessa Marcil) about his day. She goes on to tell him she is pregnant. These scenes have R-rated language.

WHAT TO WATCH FOR AND ASK YOURSELF

- Do these scenes show decision making or problem solving?
- Does Goodspeed have many problem solutions or only a few?
- Does Goodspeed's biochemistry knowledge help him choose the right solution? How does agent trainee Marvin Isherwood (Todd Louiso) respond to the situation?

CONCEPTS OR EXAMPLES

- ☐ Decision making
- ☐ Problem solving
- ☐ Lack of knowledge, experience

- ☐ Solution generation
- ☐ Solution choice
- ☐ Expert knowledge, experience

ANALYSIS

_____

_____

_____

_____

_____

_____

_____

_____

_____

_____

PERSONAL REACTIONS

_____

_____

_____

_____

_____

_____

_____

_____

_____

_____

James and the Giant Peach (II)

Color, 1996
Running Time: 1 hour, 19 minutes
Rating: G
Director: Henry Selick
Distributor: Hollywood Pictures Home Video[104]

This captivating stop-motion animated film follows a young boy's quest to leave his awful aunts and go to New York City. He discovers a giant peach on a tree in his yard. James (voiced by Paul Terry) enters it and becomes part of the diverse world of Grasshopper (voiced by Simon Callow), Centipede (voiced by Richard Dreyfuss), Ladybug (voiced by Jane Leeves), Glowworm (voiced by Miriam Margolyes), Spider (voiced by Susan Sarandon), and Earthworm (voiced by David Thewlis). This film is brilliantly animated with a captivating though bizarre story.

Note: Chapter 2 "Workforce Diversity" also discusses scenes from this film.

SCENES

DVD CHAPTER 8. PEACH ON THE MOVE TO CHAPTER 9. SHARK ATTACK! (0:26:41–0:36:03)

These scenes follow James' Aunt Spiker (Joanna Lumley) and Aunt Sponge (Miriam Margolyes) searching for him in the area around the peach. The peach has rolled through the village and fields. It lands in the ocean. The scenes start with a dark screen and a dark inside shot. You hear, "Ow! Somebody pinched me." Centipede's voice-over says, "I thought you were the spider." These scenes end after Centipede says, "New York ... Here we come!" Seagulls carry the peach aloft. The film dissolves to Earthworm moving along a wooden walkway outside the peach.

WHAT TO WATCH FOR AND ASK YOURSELF

- What problem does this group face?
- What alternatives are available to them to solve the problem?
- Does their diversity help or hinder their problem solving?

---

[104] Buena Vista Home Entertainment and Walt Disney Studios Home Entertainment also distributed this film.

CONCEPTS OR EXAMPLES

- ☐ Problem solving
- ☐ Innovation
- ☐ Options, alternatives

- ☐ Diversity and group performance
- ☐ Problem-solving group

ANALYSIS

_____

_____

_____

_____

_____

_____

_____

_____

_____

_____

PERSONAL REACTIONS

_____

_____

_____

_____

_____

_____

_____

_____

_____

_____

Papillon

Color, 1973
Running Time: 2 hours, 30 minutes
Rating: PG
Director: Franklin J. Schaffner
Distributor: Warner Home Video

This is Dalton Trumbo and Lorenzo Semple Jr.'s adaptation of the autobiographical account of Henri Charriere's repeated efforts to escape from the French prison colony on Devil's Island in the 1930s. French felon Charriere, known as "Papillon" ("Butterfly"), focused all his efforts on leaving the island, something no prisoner had ever done. Papillon (Steve McQueen) finishes his prison sentence, lives on the island, and continues to think of escape. Stock swindler Luis Dega (Dustin Hoffman) and Papillon form a close friendship during the prison ordeal.

SCENES

DVD CHAPTER 36 AN ESCAPE IDEA. TO CHAPTER 39 CODA/END CREDITS. (2:16:24–2:27:49)

These scenes close the film. Both Papillon and Dega have finished their sentences and live in cabins on Devil's Island away from the prison. Papillon has just visited Dega in Dega's cabin. These scenes begin with a shot of the surf breaking against a cliff base. The camera pans to Papillon eating a coconut and looking at the water. These scenes end after he floats away from the island. The voice-over says, "Papillon made it to freedom. And for the remaining years of his life he lived a free man." The film cuts to an abandoned prison building as the voice-over continues describing the prison in French Guiana.

WHAT TO WATCH FOR AND ASK YOURSELF

- What is the problem facing Papillon?
- What alternatives does he have to solve the problem?
- Which decision model or models best describe Papillon's decision process?

CONCEPTS OR EXAMPLES

- ☐ Problem solving
- ☐ Decision making
- ☐ Decision alternatives, options
- ☐ Decision-making process

- ☐ Garbage Can Model of decision making
- ☐ Bounded Rationality Model of decision making
- ☐ Rational Model of decision making

ANALYSIS

_____

_____

_____

_____

_____

_____

_____

_____

_____

_____

PERSONAL REACTIONS

_____

_____

_____

_____

_____

_____

_____

_____

_____

_____

CHAPTER 20

Decision Making

The **decision-making process** defines a decision problem, creates alternative courses of action, and chooses among them using specified or unspecified criteria. The criteria for choosing among alternatives can include the cost, profit, danger, or pleasure of each alternative. Although decision making focuses on choice, it also tries to reach a goal.[105]

Decision making fits within the larger context of problem-solving activities in organizations (see Chapter 19, "Problem Solving"). Individuals in organizations, especially managers, face problems, opportunities, and events requiring action. Problem solving identifies the problem, tries to find root causes, and creates the options that become input to a decision-making process. Decision making is the part of the problem-solving process that chooses a course of action.[106]

Although decision making is a basic management function, nonmanagers also make decisions.[107] The term "decision maker" refers to a person at any organizational level who picks a course of action when faced with a decision situation.

Four films offer effective scenes that show different aspects of decision making:

- *Apollo 13*
- *Butch Cassidy and the Sundance Kid*
- *My Best Friend's Wedding*
- *Network*

Apollo 13 has some superb decision-making scenes. *Butch Cassidy and the Sundance Kid* shows a major decision about whether to fight a posse or jump off a cliff into a river. *My Best Friend's Wedding* shows the stress of the decision-making process. Some closing scenes from *Network* show group decision making in action with unexpected results.

---

[105] Charles Z. Wilson and Marcus Alexis, "Basic Frameworks for Decisions," *Academy of Management Journal* 5, no. 2 (1962): 150–64.

[106] George P. Huber, *Managerial Decision Making* (Glenview, IL: Scott, Foresman and Company, 1980).

[107] Barnard, *Functions of the Executive*.

Apollo 13 (II)

Color, 1995
Running Time: 2 hours, 20 minutes
Rating: PG
Director: Ron Howard
Distributor: Universal Studios Home Video

This film shows the flight of Apollo 13, a NASA mission to the moon that almost ended in disaster. Innovative problem solving and decision making amid massive ambiguity saved the crew. Almost any scene dramatically makes this point. Flight Director Gene Kranz wrote a book describing the mission and the activities that prevented a disaster.[108] The zero gravity simulator, a KC-135 four-engine jet aircraft (NASA's "Vomit Comet"), helped create the film's realistic weightless scenes. These scenes required 600 parabolic loops over 10 days of filming.[109]

Note: Chapter 19 "Problem Solving" also discusses scenes from this film.

SCENES

DVD CHAPTER 32 FAILURE IS NOT AN OPTION (1:15:01–1:17:01)

These scenes follow the module returning to radio contact with Houston after going around the moon. They start as Flight Director Gene Kranz (Ed Harris) reaches for chalk and writes on the board. He says, "So you are telling me you can only give our guys forty-five hours." The scenes end as he leaves the room saying, "Failure is not an option."

WHAT TO WATCH FOR AND ASK YOURSELF

- Do these scenes show problem solving or decision making?
- Where is the separation between the two?
- Are these individual or group decision processes?

---

[108] Kranz, *Failure Is Not an Option*.
[109] Craddock, *VideoHound's Golden Movie Retriever*, 86.

CONCEPTS OR EXAMPLES

☐ Problem solving   ☐ Individual decision making

☐ Decision making   ☐ Group decision making

☐ Decision-making models   ☐ Decision alternatives, options

ANALYSIS

_____

_____

_____

_____

_____

_____

_____

_____

_____

PERSONAL REACTIONS

_____

_____

_____

_____

_____

_____

_____

_____

_____

Butch Cassidy and the Sundance Kid (II)

Color, 1969
Running Time: 1 hour, 51 minutes
Rating: PG
Director: George Roy Hill
Distributor: 20th Century Fox Home Entertainment

This seriocomic Western takes liberties with the lives of two legendary 1890's bank robbers. It has many memorable scenes, including a bicycle-riding scene that showcases Burt Bacharach's Oscar-winning song, "Raindrops Keep Fallin' On My Head". William Goldman's script is so sharp that you hang onto every line of dialogue. Director George Roy Hill's effort is a study of and a social commentary on the twilight of that American myth known as the Old West. Much happens along the way as a posse chases the pair, who eventually fight a large group of Bolivian police. A clever script and well-developed characters quickly made this film a classic.[110]

Note: Chapter 16 "Conflict in Organizations" also discusses scenes from this film.

SCENES

DVD CHAPTER 15 THE INDIAN, LORD BALTIMORE) THROUGH CHAPTER 17 LEAP OF FEAR (0:51:02–1:00:54)

These scenes start with Butch Cassidy (Paul Newman) and Sundance (Robert Redford) riding the same horse to escape a posse in hot pursuit. The film cuts to Butch falling into some water to cool off. He says, "Ah, you're wasting your time. They can't track us over rock." Sundance replies, "Tell them that." These scenes end as Butch and Sundance float down the river in the distance. The film cuts to a shot of Etta Place (Katherine Ross) sitting on a porch. Butch and Sundance approach the house from the screen's left.

WHAT TO WATCH FOR AND ASK YOURSELF

- Which decision-making model do Butch and Sundance follow?
- What alternatives do they assess in reaching a decision?
- Is their decision the right one under these circumstances?

---

[110] Craddock, *VideoHound's Golden Movie Retriever*, 187

CONCEPTS OR EXAMPLES

☐ Decision-making process

☐ Bounded Rationality Model of decision making

☐ Decision alternatives, options

☐ Political Decision-Making Models

☐ Rational Model of decision making

☐ Garbage Can Model of decision making

ANALYSIS

_____

_____

_____

_____

_____

_____

_____

_____

_____

PERSONAL REACTIONS

_____

_____

_____

_____

_____

_____

_____

_____

_____

_____

_____

_____

My Best Friend's Wedding (II)

Color, 1997
Running Time: 1 hour, 45 minutes
Rating: PG-13
Director: P. J. Hogan
Distributor: Columbia TriStar Home Entertainment

Sportswriter Michael O'Neal (Dermot Mulroney) and restaurant critic Julianne Potter (Julia Roberts) are best friends. They have agreed to marry each other if neither has found a partner by age 28. Michael falls for the wealthy, beautiful Kimmy (Cameron Diaz). Julianne now realizes she loves Michael and tries to stop the wedding. Her bungled efforts add great humor to the film. Beautifully photographed on location in Chicago.[111]

Note: Chapter 4 "Technology" also discusses scenes from this film.

SCENES

DVD CHAPTER 14 WALTER'S OFFICE (0:57:43–1:02:13)

These scenes start with Julianne walking down a hall toward a conference room. They follow the barge on the Chicago River scene. They end with Walter Wallace (Philip Bosco) saying goodbye to his secretary (Nydia Rodriguez Terracina). He walks toward Julianne waiting at the elevators. The film cuts to Michael and Julianne trying to unlock the front door of the Wallace Companies building.

WHAT TO WATCH FOR AND ASK YOURSELF

- What are Julianne's decision alternatives?
- What are her decision criteria?
- What effects do you predict from her decision?

---

[111] Craddock, *VideoHound's Golden Movie Retriever*, 712.

CONCEPTS OR EXAMPLES

- ☐ Decision-making process
- ☐ Decisions and stress
- ☐ Decision alternatives, options
- ☐ Unethical decision making
- ☐ Decision criteria
- ☐ Decision effects
- ☐ Ethical dilemma

ANALYSIS

_____

_____

_____

_____

_____

_____

_____

_____

_____

PERSONAL REACTIONS

_____

_____

_____

_____

_____

_____

_____

_____

_____

_____

Network (I)

Color, 1976
Running Time: 2 hours, 1 minute
Rating: R
Director: Sidney Lumet
Distributor: Warner Home Video

Union Broadcasting Systems (UBS) fires news anchor Howard Beale (Peter Finch) because of poor ratings. Max Schumacher (William Holden), News Division President, tries to soften the blow on Beale whose on-air behavior becomes increasingly bizarre. He promises to kill himself on-air—a promise that eventually makes his show a winner. Over the course of two weeks, the show's ratings skyrocket, something UBS management values over human life. The celebrated screenwriter Paddy Chayefsky wrote this scathing satire of the television industry.

**Note: Chapter 24 "Organizational Change and Development"
also discusses scenes from this film.**

SCENES

DVD CHAPTER 30 NUMBER CRUNCHERS. TO CHAPTER 31 FINAL CANCELLA-TION. (1:52:22–1:57:17)

These scenes begin with the network executives assembling in Frank Hackett's office for their decision about Howard Beale's status with the network. They follow the scene of Max Schumacher ending his affair with Diana Christensen (Faye Dunaway). Hackett (Robert Duvall) sits at his desk. The scene ends after Diana says, "I don't see we have any option, Frank. Let's kill the son of a bitch." The film intercuts several shots of the audience going into the studio with the voice-over of the discussion among the executives. The film cuts to the beginning of Howard Beale's news show.

WHAT TO WATCH FOR AND ASK YOURSELF

- What decision alternatives do these executives have?
- Which decision model guides them to a final decision?
- Is their decision ethical, unethical, legal, or illegal?

CONCEPTS OR EXAMPLES

- ☐ Decision making
- ☐ Ethical decision making
- ☐ Rational Model of decision making
- ☐ Bounded Rationality Model of decision making
- ☐ Decision-making process
- ☐ Legal decision making
- ☐ Individual decision making
- ☐ Group decision making

ANALYSIS

_____

_____

_____

_____

_____

_____

_____

_____

_____

PERSONAL REACTIONS

_____

_____

_____

_____

_____

_____

_____

_____

_____

_____

CHAPTER 21
Power and Political Behavior

Power and political behavior pervade organizational life. Each works with the other to affect people's behavior at all organizational levels.

Power is a person's ability to get something done the way the person wants it done.[112] It is the ability to affect other people's behavior and overcome resistance to changing direction. Power often is used to overcome opposition and get people to do what they otherwise might not do.[113] It includes the ability to gather physical and human resources and put them to work to reach whatever goals the person wants to reach.[114]

Political behavior in organizations focuses on getting, developing, and using power to reach a desired result in situations of uncertainty or conflict over choices. Such behavior often happens outside an organization's accepted channels of authority. You can view political behavior as unofficial, unsanctioned behavior to reach some goal.[115] People use political behavior to affect decisions, get scarce resources, and earn the cooperation of people outside their direct authority. Behavior that uses power, builds power, or tries to influence others is political.[116]

Scenes from these films show different aspects of power and political behavior:

- *Working Girl*
- *With Honors*
- *El Mariachi*
- *The Godfather*

---

[112] Gerald R. Salancik and Jeffrey Pfeffer, "Who Gets Power – And How They Hold Onto It," *Organizational Dynamics* 5, no. 3 (1977): 3–21.

[113] Jeffrey Pfeffer, *Managing with Power: Politics and Influence in Organizations* (Boston: Harvard Business School Press, 1992).

[114] Gilbert W. Fairholm, *Organizational Power Politics: Tactics in Organizational Leadership* (Santa Barbara, CA: Praeger, 2009); Rosabeth Moss Kanter, *Men and Women of the Corporation: New Edition* (New York: Basic Books, 1993).

[115] Larry E. Griener and Virginia E. Schein, *Power and Organization Development* (Reading, MA: Addison-Wesley, 1988); Dan L. Madison, et. al., "Organizational Politics: An Exploration of Managers' Perceptions," *Human Relations* 33, no. 2 (1980): 79–100; Henry Mintzberg, *Power In and Around Organizations* (Englewood Cliffs, NJ: Prentice Hall, 1983); Salancik and Pfeffer, "Who Gets Power".

[116] Bronston T. Mayes and Robert W. Allen, "Toward a Definition of Organizational Politics," *Academy of Management Review* 2, no. 4 (1977): 672–78.

The closing scenes from *Working Girl* dramatically and humorously show the meaning of political behavior in organizations. *With Honors* effectively shows three separate power relationships and the different sources of power in each. *El Mariachi* shows different aspects of sources of power, although with some violence. The scenes from *The Godfather* are dramatic, nonviolent portrayals of power and political behavior.

Working Girl

Color, 1988
Running Time: 1 hour, 55 minutes
Rating: R
Director: Mike Nichols
Distributor: 20th Century Fox Home Entertainment

Tess McGill (Melanie Griffith) continually tries to move from a secretary's position to a management position. She is not successful after several efforts. Her boss Katherine Parker (Sigourney Weaver) breaks her leg in a skiing accident, creating an opportunity for Tess to take over her job temporarily. Tess develops some good ideas for an acquisition by Trask Industries. Jack Trainer (Harrison Ford), an investment banker, helps Tess present the proposal but Katherine returns to take it as her own. The American Film Institute ranks this film in the top 100 cinema love stories.[117]

SCENES

DVD CHAPTER 17. CAUGHT TO CHAPTER 19. ANOTHER CHANCE (1:37:06–1:45:07)

These scenes start with Tess clearing her desk and saying goodbye to her coworkers. They follow the scenes of Tess on the ferry crossing to Manhattan. The scenes end when she accepts Oren Trask's (Philip Bosco) job offer. Tess and Jack embrace while her former coworkers applaud. The film cuts to Tess and Jack having breakfast and making lunch before going to work.

WHAT TO WATCH FOR AND ASK YOURSELF

- What is Tess McGill's power base?
- Is Tess working within or outside her normal reporting relationships?
- Is there a power shift in these scenes? Does anyone gain or lose power?

---

[117] Germain, "'Casablanca' Top Romance Film".

CONCEPTS OR EXAMPLES

☐ Bases of power   ☐ Political strategy

☐ Power   ☐ Power dynamics

☐ Power dimensions   ☐ Power loss

☐ Political behavior   ☐ Power gain

ANALYSIS

_____

_____

_____

_____

_____

_____

_____

_____

_____

PERSONAL REACTIONS

_____

_____

_____

_____

_____

_____

_____

_____

_____

_____

With Honors

Color, 1994
Running Time: 1 hour, 40 minutes
Rating: PG-13
Director: Alek Keshishian
Distributor: Warner Home Video

Harvard senior, Monty Kessler (Brendan Fraser) loses the only copy of his undergraduate thesis. It falls into the hands of street bum Simon Wilder (Joe Pesci). Simon is willing to return it, one page at a time, in exchange for favors such as food, clothing, and a place to live. Simon is feisty and perceives himself as no ordinary bum. "I'm a bum. But ... I'm a Harvard bum," Simon says later in the film. He becomes entangled in the lives of Monty and his roommates. Monty and Simon develop a close relationship as the film unfolds.

SCENES

DVD CHAPTER 1 ARISE, FAIR HARVARD THROUGH CHAPTER 4 A BARGAIN IN THE BASEMENT. (0:02:29–0:12:47)

These scenes start with disk jockey Everett (Patrick Dempsey) saying, "Now here's something to crow about." They follow the scenes of Monty jogging and running through Courtney's (Moira Kelly) Harvard Crew team. The scenes end when Monty leaves Widner Library and meets Courtney outside. She says, "You didn't get it?" They leave to return to their house. The film cuts to Courtney examining donuts under a magnifying glass.

WHAT TO WATCH FOR AND ASK YOURSELF

- What are the bases of power in the relationships among Monty, Professor Pitkannan (Gore Vidal), Courtney, the security guard (Marshall Hambro), and Simon?
- Which dimensions of power relationships do the scenes show?
- Does Simon behave ethically or unethically?

CONCEPTS OR EXAMPLES

☐ Power

☐ Bases of power (individual, organizational)

☐ Sources of power

☐ Ethical or unethical behavior

☐ Power relationships

☐ Dimensions of power relationships

☐ Facets of power (actual, potential, potential for)

ANALYSIS

_____

_____

_____

_____

_____

_____

_____

_____

_____

PERSONAL REACTIONS

_____

_____

_____

_____

_____

_____

_____

_____

_____

_____

_____

El Mariachi

Color, 1993
Spanish with English subtitles
Running Time: 1 hour, 21 minutes
Rating: R
Director: Robert Rodriguez
Distributor: Columbia TriStar Home Video

El Mariachi (Carlos Gallardo) wants to be a *mariachi* (traveling musician), as were his great-grandfather, grandfather, and father. His guitar case and black clothing cause him to be misidentified as Azul (Reinol Martinez), an enemy of drug lord Moco (Peter Marquardt).

The story about making this film is as enjoyable as the film. First time director Robert Rodriguez stayed in a research hospital to raise money to make the film. He and his crew of family, relatives, and cast shot it on a $7,000 budget in eleven consecutive days with no re-takes, using borrowed equipment. The closing credits are among the most amusing to watch in cinema. Rodriquez remade this film on a studio budget as *Desperado* (1995), also known as *El Mariachi 2*.[118]

SCENES

DVD CHAPTER 1. START (0:00:14–0:07:09)

These scenes start the film after the Columbia Pictures logo and a dark screen. They begin with a shot of a disabled jeep with "SEGURIDAD PUBLICA" (public safety) written on its door. The film cuts to a sign on a building wall that reads, "CARCEL PUBLICA" (public jail). A police van arrives. These scenes end after the screen goes black followed by the text screen, "Columbia Pictures Presents."

WHAT TO WATCH FOR AND ASK YOURSELF

- What are the bases of power of the jail guards?
- What are the bases of power of the prisoners?
- What are the bases of power of the gunmen?

---

[118] Craddock, *VideoHound's Golden Movie Retriever*, 337.

CONCEPTS OR EXAMPLES

- ☐ Power
- ☐ Bases of power (individual, organizational)
- ☐ Power relationships
- ☐ Facets of power (actual, potential, potential for)
- ☐ Dimensions of power and power relationships

ANALYSIS

_____

_____

_____

_____

_____

_____

_____

_____

_____

PERSONAL REACTIONS

_____

_____

_____

_____

_____

_____

_____

_____

_____

The Godfather (III)

Color, 1972
Running Time: 2 hours, 51 minutes
Rating: R
Director: Francis Ford Coppola
Distributor: Paramount Home Video

This film, based on Mario Puzo's novel, is a powerful look at a Mafia family led by Don Corleone (Marlon Brando). It is an intense film that roams through the personal lives of its characters and shows the fiercely violent side of organized crime. The film suggests stunning parallels between managing a gangster organization and managing an organization of any other type. An irresistible work, *The Godfather* is filled with memorable scenes and memorable performances. The American Film Institute in 1998 ranked this film in the top 100 American films.[119]

Note: Chapter 6 "Ethics and Behavior in Organizations" and Chapter 10 "Organizational Culture" also discuss scenes from this film.

SCENES

DVD CHAPTER 17. WE ARE ALL REASONABLE MEN HERE (2:06:01–2:12:49)

The scenes follow Michael Corleone's (Al Pacino) preparations to return to the United States from Sicily. A car bomb has just killed his wife Apollonia (Simonetta Stefanelli). These scenes start with an upward panning shot of a building and cut to Barzini (Richard Conte) with Don Corleone's voice-over, "Don Barzini, I want to thank you for helping me organize this meeting here today." The scenes end as Tom Hagen (Robert Duvall) and Corleone are riding in a car. Coreleone says, "But I didn't know until this day that it was... Barzini all along." The car continues into the night as the film fades to an outside shot of a school.

WHAT TO WATCH FOR AND ASK YOURSELF

- What are Don Corleone's sources and bases of power?
- What are the sources and bases of power of the other family heads?
- What facets of power appear in these scenes?

---

[119] Craddock, *VideoHound's Golden Movie Retriever*, 429.

CONCEPTS OR EXAMPLES

☐ Power

☐ Sources of power

☐ Bases of power (individual, organizational)

☐ Facets of power (actual, potential, potential for)

☐ Power relationships

☐ Dimensions of power and power relationships

☐ Attribution of power

ANALYSIS

_____

_____

_____

_____

_____

_____

_____

_____

PERSONAL REACTIONS

_____

_____

_____

_____

_____

_____

_____

_____

_____

CHAPTER 22
Stress in Organizations

S tress is an unavoidable feature of life, a worldwide phenomenon that appears in many cultures. A person experiences **stress** when the environment presents a constraint, an opportunity, or an excessive physical or psychological demand.[120]

The words **stressor** or **stressors** refer to objects or events in a person's physical and social environment that can induce a stress response. Stressors can occur in any environment through which a person passes. Those environments include the work environment, the nonwork environment, and the surrounding social, economic, and cultural environment.

The **stress response** is a complex process that prepares the body to respond to a stressor. A person's perceptual process affects whether the presence of a stressor leads to a stress response. One person may perceive a stressor as a challenge to overcome; another person may perceive the same stressor as a threat. The stress response leads either to **distress** (negative result) or **eustress** (positive result).

Stress is not always bad. Some stress can energize and motivate a person to behave in desired ways. It can move a person toward valued results offered by an opportunity.

The following films have humorous or dramatic portrayals of stress, stressors, and stress responses.

- *Head Office*
- *Broadcast News*
- *The Paper*
- *Falling Down*

---

[120] Terry A. Beehr, *Psychological Stress in the Workplace* (New York: Routledge, 1999); Cary L. Cooper, Philip J. Dewe, and Michael P. O'Driscoll, *Organizational Stress: A Review and Critique of Theory, Research, and Applications* (Thousand Oaks, CA: Sage Publications, Inc., 2001); M. Blake Hargrove, James C. Quick, Debra L. Nelson, and Jonathan D. Quick, "The Theory of Preventive Stress Management: A 33-year Review and Evaluation," *Stress and Health* 27, no. 3 (2011): 182–93; Ronald Glaser and Janice Kiecolt-Glaser, *Handbook of Human Stress and Immunity* (San Diego: Academic Press, 1994); Michael T. Matteson and John M. Ivancevich, "Organizational Stressors and Heart Disease: A Research Model," *Academy of Management Review* 4, no. 3 (1979): 347–57; James C. Quick and Jonathan D. Quick, *Organizational Stress and Preventive Management* (New York: McGraw-Hill, 1984); Hans Selye, "The Stress Concept: Past, Present, and Future," in *Stress Research*, ed. Cary L. Cooper (New York: John Wiley & Sons, 1983), 1–19.

Head Office presents stress and the stress response in a hysterically comical way. *Broadcast News* has dramatic scenes showing distress and eustress results. *The Paper* shows how work and nonwork roles interact to cause a stress response. The Los Angeles traffic jam scenes in *Falling Down* feature multiple sources of stressors.

Head Office

Color, 1986
Running Time: 1 hour, 30 minutes
Rating PG-13
Director: Ken Finkleman
Distributor: HBO Home Video

This film presents a comic-satirical view of power and political behavior at an organization's highest levels. Confusion surrounds the unexpectedly fast promotions of Jack Issel (Judge Reinhold). This lighthearted film offers many observations on corporate life, including stress, power, political behavior, and ethics.

SCENES

DVD CHAPTER 2. NEW RECRUIT (0:08:22–0:11:50)

These scenes begin with Frank Stedman (Danny DeVito) reacting to the SEC investigation reported in the *Financial Weekly* (Stedman refers to it as "The Journal."). The scenes end after Jane (Jane Seymour) reneges on a date with Stedman for that evening. Jane walks off as Stedman mutters, "Count on ya? Ha. Ha."

WHAT TO WATCH FOR AND ASK YOURSELF

- What stressors affect Stedman? Can he remove them from his environment?
- Is Stedman experiencing the stress response? What evidence of the stress response appears in these scenes?
- Do these scenes show distress (negative response) or eustress (positive response)?

CONCEPTS OR EXAMPLES

☐ Stress

☐ Stressors

☐ Stress response (physiological, psychological)

☐ Stress results

☐ Distress (negative response)

☐ "Fight or flight" response

☐ Eustress (positive response)

ANALYSIS

_____

_____

_____

_____

_____

_____

_____

_____

_____

_____

PERSONAL REACTIONS

_____

_____

_____

_____

_____

_____

_____

_____

_____

_____

Broadcast News (III)

Color, 1987
Running Time: 2 hours, 12 minutes
Rating: R
Director: James L. Brooks
Distributor: 20ᵗʰ Century Fox Home Entertainment

This romantic comedy features three well-defined and sharply different personalities. The opening scenes show their early personality development within their families.

Each character has different personality characteristics. Jane Craig (Holly Hunter), a bright, driven, compulsive news producer; Tom Grunich (William Hurt), a smooth, modern news anchor; and Aaron Altman (Albert Brooks), a veteran reporter who reacts jealously to Tom's on-camera success. The romantic triangle among these characters adds a strong comedic flavor to the film.

Note: Chapter 9 "Personality" and Chapter 12 "Motivation:
Need Theories" also discuss scenes from this film.

SCENES

DVD CHAPTER 5. INSECURITY AND DESPERATION THROUGH CHAPTER 6. BILL SMILED! (0:20:28–0:24:48)

These scenes start in the editing room. The lead-in sound-over is the squeal of a rewinding tape. The scenes follow the hallway ethics discussion between Aaron and other station staff members. They end after Aaron reviews the end of the tape with Bobby (Christian Clemenson) the tape editor and says, "He did smile." The film cuts to the newsroom with Jane and Tom talking. These scenes contrast nicely with the *Head Office* scenes (pp. 200-201).

WHAT TO WATCH FOR AND ASK YOURSELF

* What do these scenes suggest about the stress response's role in a person's behavior?
* Do the scenes show distress (negative response), eustress (positive response), or both?
* Does success with the project help them recover from the stress response?

CONCEPTS OR EXAMPLES

☐ Stress

☐ Distress (negative response)

☐ Stressors

☐ Sources of stress (work, nonwork, life transition)

☐ Stress results

☐ Eustress (positive response)

☐ Stress response (physiological, psychological)

ANALYSIS

_____

_____

_____

_____

_____

_____

_____

_____

_____

PERSONAL REACTIONS

_____

_____

_____

_____

_____

_____

_____

_____

_____

The Paper

Color, 1994
Running Time: 1 hour, 52 minutes
Rating: R
Director: Ron Howard
Distributor: Universal Studios Home Video

This engaging film shows the ethical dilemmas and stress of producing *The New York Sun*, a daily metropolitan newspaper. Henry Hackett (Michael Keaton) races against the clock to publish a story about a major police scandal that could send two young African American men to jail. He is in constant conflict with Managing Editor, Alicia Clark (Glenn Close), who focuses more on budget control than running accurate stories. Hackett also feels constant pressure from his wife, Marty (Marisa Tomei), who is pregnant with their first child. While Hackett tries to get the story he wants, Marty urges him to take a less demanding job at *The Sentinel*.[121]

SCENES

DVD CHAPTER 6 HASSLING HENRY (0:35:30–0:39:44)

These scenes begin with Henry Hackett walking through the newsroom and entering his office. He finds Dan McDougall (Randy Quaid) lying on his sofa. The scenes follow the office discussion between Alicia and Bernie White (Robert Duvall) in White's office. They end after McDougall says to Henry and Marty, "You two take your time. I'm on the Sedona thing." He leaves the office and closes the door. Marty says, "God, I miss this place." The film cuts to a close-up of a box of donuts. These scenes have several instances of R-rated language.

WHAT TO WATCH FOR AND ASK YOURSELF

- What are the sources of stressors affecting Henry Hackett?
- How could Henry manage the stress in his life?
- Do stressors from different sources affect each other or are they insulated from each other?

---

[121] Champoux, "Seeing and Valuing Diversity."

CONCEPTS OR EXAMPLES

☐ Stress

☐ Stressors

☐ Stress results

☐ Sources of stressors (work, nonwork, life transitions)

☐ Distress (negative result)

☐ Eustress (positive result)

☐ Stress response (physiological, psychological)

☐ Perceived stress

ANALYSIS

_____

_____

_____

_____

_____

_____

_____

_____

_____

PERSONAL REACTIONS

_____

_____

_____

_____

_____

_____

_____

_____

_____

Falling Down

Color, 1993
Running Time: 1 hour, 53 minutes
Rating: R
Director: Joel Schumacher
Distributor: *Warner Home Video*

Bill "D-FENS" Foster (Michael Douglas), a law-abiding white-collar worker, snaps while stuck in a Los Angeles freeway traffic jam on a hot day. Facing the stressors of divorce and unemployment, he leaves his car and goes on a violent rage lashing at anyone who gets in his way. This film has many harrowing moments as Foster tries, by force, to return to the happy, normal life he never really had. His pursuer, Detective Pendergast (Robert Duvall), has one day before retirement but sets out to capture him.

SCENES

DVD CHAPTER 1 (0:00:35–0:04:55)

These scenes start at the film's beginning during the opening credits. They begin after the title screen, "A Joel Schumacher Film." The camera slowly pulls back from a close-up of Foster's perspiring face. The scenes end after Foster runs off into the shrubs under the highway overpass. The film cuts to Detective Pendergast sitting in his patrol car.

WHAT TO WATCH FOR AND ASK YOURSELF

- What stressors affect Bill Foster?
- What are his physiological and psychological stress responses?
- Does Foster experience eustress (positive result) or distress (negative result)?

CONCEPTS OR EXAMPLES

- ☐ Stressors
- ☐ Stress response
- ☐ Physiological stress response

- ☐ Psychological stress response
- ☐ Eustress (positive result)
- ☐ Distress (negative result)

ANALYSIS

_____

_____

_____

_____

_____

_____

_____

_____

_____

PERSONAL REACTIONS

_____

_____

_____

_____

_____

_____

_____

_____

_____

_____

CHAPTER 23
Organizational Design

Organizational design refers to the way managers structure their organization to reach organizational goals. The allocation of duties, tasks, and responsibilities between departments and individuals are parts of organizational design. Reporting relationships and the number of levels in the organization's hierarchy are other structural elements.[122]

Organizational charts show an organization's formal design. They show the configuration of the organization as it is or as managers want it. Such charts typically use boxes to show organizational positions and lines connecting the boxes to show reporting relationships.[123]

The **goals of organizational design** are: (1) it must get information to the right places for effective decision making, and (2) it must help coordinate the organization's interdependent parts. When the organization's design is not right for what it is doing, managers may not get the information they need to predict problems and make effective decisions.[124] They also may not react quickly enough to problems because the existing organizational design blocks needed information. Conflict levels in the organization could be excessively high, implying misalignments in the organization's design.

This chapter discusses scenes from the following films:

- *The River Wild*
- *The Hudsucker Proxy*
- *The Hunt for Red October*
- *The Dirty Dozen*

---

[122] David K. Banner and T. Elaine Gagné, *Designing Effective Organizations: Traditional & Transformational Views* (Thousand Oaks, CA: Sage Publications, 1991); Richard J. Butler, *Designing Organizations: A Decision-Making Perspective* (New York: Routledge, 1991); Margaret R. Davis and David A. Weckler, *A Practical Guide to Organization Design* (Menlo Park, CA: Crisp Publications, 1996); Eric G. Flamholtz and Yvonne Randle, *Changing the Game: Organizational Transformations of the First, Second, and Third Kinds* (New York: Oxford University Press, 1998); David A. Nadler and Michael L. Tushman (with Mark B. Nadler), *Competing by Design: The Power of Organizational Architecture* (New York: Oxford University Press, 1997.)

[123] Karol K. White, *Understanding the Company Organization Chart* (New York: American Management Association, 1963).

[124] Robert Duncan, "What Is the Right Organization Structure? Decision Tree Analysis Provides the Answer," *Organizational Dynamics* 7, no. 3 (1979): 59–80.

The white water river rafting scenes from *The River Wild* are excellent visual metaphors for turbulent external environments. *The Hudsucker Proxy* shows a functional organizational design in action. *The Hunt for Red October* shows different functional areas of a submarine working to reach its mission. *The Dirty Dozen* effectively shows strategy formation and a resulting organizational design.

The River Wild

Color, 1994
Running Time: 1 hour, 52 minutes
Rating: PG-13
Director: Curtis Hanson
Distributor: Universal Studios Home Video

Two crooks, psychopath Wade (Kevin Bacon) and his partner Terry (John C. Riley), start down the river in a rubber raft. A chance meeting with Gail (Meryl Streep) and her family changes the family's vacation dramatically. Wade has a gun but quickly learns that he and Terry must depend on Gail, an experienced river guide, to safely get through the rapids. The most challenging stretch of rapids is The Gauntlet, the convergence of three rivers, and a drop of 295 feet in one and a half miles. This film gives you the added experience of beautiful Oregon and Montana views.[125]

SCENES

DVD CHAPTER 13 THE RIVER WILD (1:34:16–1:40:55)

This sequence appears near the film's end during their difficult river trip. It includes intercut scenes of Gail's husband Tom (David Strathairn) setting up a trap downstream. The sequence starts as the raft carrying Wade, Terry, Gail, and her son Roarke (Joseph Mazzello) approaches The Gauntlet. Gail has said, "Vacation's over." It ends after they pass through the last rapids and cheer their success. The film cuts to the raft approaching Tom's trap. This sequence has one instance of R-rated language.

WHAT TO WATCH FOR AND ASK YOURSELF

- What type of environment do the four people in the raft face?
- Does their environment change as they go through The Gauntlet?
- If so, do they change their organizational design?

---

[125] Craddock, *VideoHound's Golden Movie Retriever*, 858.

CONCEPTS OR EXAMPLES

- ☐ External environment
- ☐ Dynamic environment
- ☐ Stable environment

- ☐ Turbulent environment
- ☐ Simple, static external environment
- ☐ Complex, dynamic external environment

ANALYSIS

_____

_____

_____

_____

_____

_____

_____

_____

PERSONAL REACTIONS

_____

_____

_____

_____

_____

_____

_____

_____

_____

The Hudsucker Proxy (II)

Color, 1994
Running Time: 1 hour, 51 minutes
Rating: PG
Director: Joel Coen
Distributor: Warner Home Video

Norville Barnes (Tim Robbins), a graduate of the Muncie College of Business Administration, quickly moves from mailroom clerk to president of Hudsucker Industries. The board of directors appoints him in the hope that his incompetence will drive down the stock price so they can buy a controlling interest. Norville has his own idea for a product, a simple plastic hoop. After a slow start in sales, the hula hoop becomes a success, drives the stock price up, and causes the board great distress. Sidney J. Mussburger (Paul Newman) aspires to the presidency and sabotages Norville by presenting him as insane. The film takes a delightful twist at the end. Norville inherits the late Waring Hudsucker's fortune, regains the presidency, and presents the board with a new product idea—the Frisbee®.

Note: Chapter 11 "Organizational Socialization" also discusses scenes from this film.

SCENES

DVD CHAPTER 23 NORVILLE'S DINGUS. TO CHAPTER 25 JUMPING THROUGH HOOPS. (0:59:45–1:04:47)

The scenes start with a woman saying "Shh!" to the camera. It zooms to a sign on the boardroom door that reads, "Quiet Please! Board Meeting in Session." These scenes follow Norville's romantic evening with Amy Archer (Jennifer Jason Leigh). They end after the hula hoop sign appears in a toy store window and the store owner steps outside. The film cuts to Norville Barnes' office and Amy looking at a ticker tape.

WHAT TO WATCH FOR AND ASK YOURSELF

- Which types of organizational design do these scenes show?
- Which organizational design characteristics appear in these scenes?
- Do these scenes show any behavioral demands of organizational design? What are they?

CONCEPTS OR EXAMPLES

- ☐ Organizational design by division
- ☐ Organizational design by function
- ☐ Hybrid organizational design

- ☐ Matrix organizational design

- ☐ Process view of organizational design
- ☐ Simple, static external environment
- ☐ Complex, dynamic external environment
- ☐ Self-managing teams

ANALYSIS

_____

_____

_____

_____

_____

_____

_____

_____

_____

PERSONAL REACTIONS

_____

_____

_____

_____

_____

_____

_____

_____

_____

_____

The Hunt for Red October (II)

Color, 1990
Running Time: 2 hours, 15 minutes
Rating: PG
Director: John McTiernan
Distributor: Paramount Home Entertainment

This film is an intense story of the search for the Soviet submarine *Red October*. Contradictory information says its commander Captain Marko Ramius (Sean Connery) is either defecting to the United States or has gone berserk and will unleash nuclear missiles on the U.S. The Soviets want the U.S. to find the *Red October* and destroy it. CIA agent Dr. Jack Ryan (Alec Baldwin) believes Ramius wants to defect and does not want him killed.

Note: Chapter 10 "Organizational Culture" also discusses scenes from this film.

SCENES

DVD CHAPTER 9 RENDEZVOUS (1:27:06–1:36:45)

These scenes start with Russian Ambassador Andrei Lysenko (Joss Ackland) saying to Jeffrey Pelt (Richard Jordan), the President's National Security Adviser, "I have to talk to the President." They follow the scenes of Ryan boarding the submarine *U.S.S. Dallas*. The scenes end after Captain Mancuso (Scott Glenn) says, "He wants to go up and take a peek. We'll play along." The film cuts to both submarines going to the surface.

WHAT TO WATCH FOR AND ASK YOURSELF

- Which forms of organizational design do these scenes show?
- Are the forms as clean and pure in practice as implied by these scenes?
- Do these organizational forms help the two submarines reach their mission?

CONCEPTS OR EXAMPLES

- ☐ Organizational design by division
- ☐ Organizational design by function
- ☐ Hybrid organizational design

- ☐ Matrix organizational design

- ☐ Process view of organizational design
- ☐ Simple, static external environment
- ☐ Complex, dynamic external environment
- ☐ Self-managing teams

ANALYSIS

_____

_____

_____

_____

_____

_____

_____

_____

_____

PERSONAL REACTIONS

_____

_____

_____

_____

_____

_____

_____

_____

_____

The Dirty Dozen (II)

Color, 1967
Running Time: 2 hours, 29 minutes
Rating: NR
Director: Robert Aldrich
Distributor: Warner Home Video

Army Major Reisman (Lee Marvin) has the almost impossible task of developing a team of twelve men for action behind the lines against the Germans in World War II. He recruits his men from the murderers, thieves, and rapists in an army prison and makes a deal with them: successfully complete the mission and the army will commute their sentences. The mission: parachute behind enemy lines at night and blow up a chateau full of German officers before D-Day.

Note: Chapter 15 "Groups and Intergroup Processes" also discusses scenes from this film.

SCENES

DVD CHAPTER 22 THE LAST SUPPER (1:41:16–1:44:07)

These scenes start with a close-up of Jimenez (Trini Lopez) banging a spoon on a wine bottle to get the group's attention. He says, "Hey Major!" The Dirty Dozen has just successfully taken Colonel Breed's (Robert Ryan) headquarters during maneuvers. A sumptuous dinner is their reward. The scenes end after Major Reisman begins another review of the plan. He says, "All right, let's take it again from the top without all the ad libs." The film cuts to the Dirty Dozen aboard a transport aircraft with Reisman continuing to review the plan.

WHAT TO WATCH FOR AND ASK YOURSELF

- Does Major Reisman's strategy lead to a specific organizational design?
- If *yes*, what are its key features?
- What type of environment will the Dirty Dozen face while carrying out their plan?

CONCEPTS OR EXAMPLES

☐ Contingency factors of organizational design

☐ External environment

☐ Complex, dynamic external environment

☐ Environmental uncertainty

☐ Strategy (strategic planning)

☐ Roles

☐ Role Relationships

☐ Functional organizational design

☐ Simple, static external environment

ANALYSIS

_____

_____

_____

_____

_____

_____

_____

_____

PERSONAL REACTIONS

_____

_____

_____

_____

_____

_____

_____

_____

_____

CHAPTER 24
Organizational Change and Development

Organizational change involves movement from an organization's present state to a future or target state.[126] The future state can include a new organizational strategy, changes in the organization's culture, introduction of a new technology, and so on.

Organizational change is either unplanned or planned. **Unplanned change** occurs when pressures for change overwhelm efforts to resist the change. Management may not expect such change, resulting in uncontrolled change effects. **Planned change** is a systematic effort to move an organization, or a subsystem, to a new state. Planned change includes deliberately changing the organization's design, technology, tasks, people, information systems, and the like.

A consultant often serves as a **change agent** to help managers bring about planned organizational change. The consultant may be external to the organization or part of an internal staff function that specializes in helping managers carry out planned organizational change.

Scenes from the following films show different aspects of organizational change and development:

- *The Coca-Cola Kid*
- *The Company Men*
- *Network*
- *The Efficiency Expert*

The *Coca-Cola Kid*, an Australian film, shows a change agent who is not right for the target of change. Two sets of scenes from *The Company Men* show the effects of termination from work on a person and his family. *Network* shows some behavioral effects of a proposed organizational change. *The Efficiency Expert* shows some worker effects of organizational change and the consultant's reaction to those effects.

---

126 Richard Beckhard and Reuben T. Harris, *Organizational Transitions: Managing Complex Change*, 2nd ed. (Reading, MA: Addison-Wesley Publishing Company, Inc., 1991); Richard Beckhard and Wendy Pritchard, *Changing the Essence: The Art of Creating and Leading Fundamental Change in Organizations* (San Francisco: Jossey-Bass, 1992); Michael Beer and Anna Elise Walton, "Organizational Change and Development," in *Annual Review of Psychology*, 38, ed. Mark R. Rosenzweig and Lyman W. Porter (Stanford, CA: Annual Reviews, 1987), 339–67; W. Warner Burke, "Organization Change: What We Know, What We Need to Know," *Journal of Management Inquiry* 4, no. 2 (1995): 158–71; Leonard D. Goodstein and W. Warner Burke, "Creating Successful Organizational Change," *Organizational Dynamics* 19, no. 4 (1991): 5–17.

The Coca-Cola Kid

Color, 1985
Running Time: 1 hour, 34 minutes
Rating: R
Director: Dušan Makavejev
Distributor: MGM Home Entertainment

This Australian film shows Becker's (Eric Roberts) frustrated efforts to bring an old soft drink bottling plant into modern times. T. George McDowell (Bill Kerr) resists Becker's efforts to convert him to manufacturing Coca-Cola. This comedy shows some wonderful footage of Australia and features a satirical look at Australian organizations and management practices. Yugoslavian director Dušan Makavejev created an international film with no boundaries. He recruited a British actress (Terri, Greta Scacchi), Australian screenwriter Frank Moorhouse, and an American actor (Roberts).

SCENES

DVD CHAPTER 9. "CALL ME T. GEORGE" (0:36:42–0:41:31)

These scenes start with a shot of McDowell's face on a sign above a plant building. T. George's face rears up on the screen as Becker arrives at the plant. Becker drags Bushman (Tony Barry), McDowell's hired killer, behind the jeep. They follow the scenes of Becker's encounter with Bushman while traveling to the plant. These scenes end as Becker drives away after his discussion with McDowell. The film cuts to a shot of a parrot.

WHAT TO WATCH FOR AND ASK YOURSELF

- Is Becker's approach to changing McDowell's factory likely to lead to major change?
- How should Becker approach McDowell?
- What do you predict is the result of Becker's change efforts?

CONCEPTS OR EXAMPLES

- ☐ Organizational change
- ☐ Resistance to change
- ☐ Reasons for resistance
- ☐ Change target
- ☐ Change agent
- ☐ Change agent characteristics

ANALYSIS

_____

_____

_____

_____

_____

_____

_____

_____

_____

PERSONAL REACTIONS

_____

_____

_____

_____

_____

_____

_____

_____

_____

_____

The Company Men

Color, 2010
Running Time: 1 hour, 45 minutes
Rating: R
Director: John Wells
Distributor: Anchor Bay Entertainment

Three executives of GTX Global Transportation Systems face termination as the company downsizes to stay competitive. Bobby Walker (Ben Affleck) is the first to go and faces serious disruption to his previously affluent life style. Gene McClary (Tommy Lee Jones) and Phil Woodward (Chris Cooper) follow as the next casualties also affecting their family life with especially negative effects on Woodward.

SCENES

There are two sets of scenes showing the effects of organizational change on Walker and his family. The first set shows the termination action. The second set shows the beginning of the family effects.

DVD CHAPTER 1 (0:01:49–0:04:13)

These scenes start with Walker entering the GTX lobby. He says "Good morning" to the receptionist. They end with him entering Gene's office and asking about him. The scenes have one instance of R-rated language.

DVD CHAPTER 3 (0:10:10–0:12:19)

These scenes follow McClary's discussion with GTX CEO James Salinger (Craig T. Nelson) about closing the Mobile and Newport News shipyards. Maggie (Rosemarie DeWitt), Walker's wife, unloads some bags from her car and enters the house. The scenes end after Walker asks Maggie to not tell anyone. The film cuts to Woodward entering his driveway. These scenes also have some R-rated language.

WHAT TO WATCH FOR AND ASK YOURSELF

- Is Walker's termination a form of organizational change for GTX?
- What specific effects on Walker do you expect from this organizational change?
- What effect can this change have on Walker's family?

Joseph E. Champoux

CONCEPTS OR EXAMPLES

- [ ] Organizational change
- [ ] Termination as dramatic organizational change
- [ ] Effects on personal life
- [ ] Effects on family life

ANALYSIS

_____

_____

_____

_____

_____

_____

_____

_____

_____

_____

_____

PERSONAL REACTIONS

_____

_____

_____

_____

_____

_____

_____

_____

_____

_____

Network (II)

Color, 1976
Running Time: 2 hours, 1 minute
Rating: R
Director: Sidney Lumet
Distributor: Warner Home Video

Union Broadcasting Systems (UBS) fires news anchor Howard Beale (Peter Finch) because of poor ratings. Max Schumacher (William Holden), News Division President, tries to soften the blow on Beale. His on-air behavior becomes increasingly bizarre after he promises to kill himself on-air—a promise that eventually makes his show a winner. Over the course of two weeks, the show's ratings skyrocket, something UBS management values over human life. The celebrated screenwriter Paddy Chayefsky wrote this scathing satire of the television industry.

Note: Chapter 20 "Decision Making" also discusses scenes from this film.

SCENES

DVD CHAPTER 6 NO MORE BULL. TO CHAPTER 7 SAYING WHAT THEY FEEL. (0:16:15–0:22:30)

These scenes follow a meeting in Diana Christensen's (Faye Dunaway) office. They begin with the opening of the board of directors meeting. Frank Hackett (Robert Duvall) says, "But the business of management is management." The scenes end after Edward Ruddy (William Prince), president of the Systems Group, sits in a chair rubbing his brow. He asks to see Howard Beale. The film cuts to Howard Beale's news conference. These scenes have some R-rated language.

WHAT TO WATCH FOR AND ASK YOURSELF

- Does Hackett propose a major change in the organization's design?
- Is there evidence of resistance to change?
- How could they manage the change process to maximize any change's positive effects?

CONCEPTS OR EXAMPLES

- ☐ Organizational change
- ☐ Organizational design
- ☐ Behavioral effects of organizational design

- ☐ Resistance to change
- ☐ Managing to reduce resistance to change

ANALYSIS

_____

_____

_____

_____

_____

_____

_____

_____

_____

_____

PERSONAL REACTIONS

_____

_____

_____

_____

_____

_____

_____

_____

_____

_____

The Efficiency Expert

Color, 1992
Running Time: 1 hour, 37 minutes
Rating: PG
Director: Mark Joffe
Distributor: Miramax Films

Balls Moccasin Company in Spotswood, Australia is losing money. A company interested in acquiring it sends a consultant to assess its condition and help it improve operations. The company's president has sold assets over the years to cover its losses. Set in 1960s Australia, this film released in Australia and some other countries as *Spotswood*.[127]

SCENES

DVD CHAPTER 8. KIM AND CAREY (0:46:27–0:50:34)

These scenes open on a Balls Moccasins sign on a car door. They follow Kim's (Russell Crowe) jealous rage against Cary (Ben Mendelsohn). These scenes end after Cary examines his flat bicycle tire. The film cuts to a worker protest march.

WHAT TO WATCH FOR AND ASK YOURSELF

- What are the effects of Mr. Wallace's (Sir Anthony Hopkins) change efforts?
- What information could Wallace and Mr. Ball (Alwyn Kurts) learn from employee reactions to the changes?
- How could the consultant and management have reduced resistance to change?

---

[127] Craddock, *VideoHound's Golden Movie Retriever*, 335.

CONCEPTS OR EXAMPLES

- ☐ Organizational change effects
- ☐ Organizational change
- ☐ Change agent
- ☐ Reaction to change

- ☐ Resistance to change
- ☐ Information from resistance
- ☐ Reducing resistance to change

ANALYSIS

_____

_____

_____

_____

_____

_____

_____

_____

PERSONAL REACTIONS

_____

_____

_____

_____

_____

_____

_____

_____

Bibliography

Aho, C. Michael, and Sylvia Ostry. "Regional Trading Blocs: Pragmatic or Problematic Policy?" In *The Global Economy: America's Role in the Decade Ahead.* Edited by William Emerson Brock and Robert D. Hormats. New York: W. W. Norton, 1990, 147–173.

Alderfer, Clayton P. *Existence, Relatedness, and Growth: Human Needs in Organizational Settings.* New York: Free Press, 1972.

Allen, Robert F., and Saul Pilnick. "Confronting the Shadow Organization: How to Detect and Defeat Negative Norms." *Organizational Dynamics* 1, no. 4 (1973): 6–10.

Allport, Gordon W. *Personality: A Psychological Interpretation.* New York: Henry Holt, 1937.

Alvesson, Mats, and Per-Olaf Berg. *Corporate Culture and Organizational Symbolism.* New York: Hawthorne/Walter de Gruyter, 1992.

Ballesteros, Soledad. "Cognitive Approaches to Human Perception: Introduction." In *Cognitive Approaches to Human Perception*, chap. 1. Edited by Soledad Ballesteros. Hillsdale, NJ: Lawrence Erlbaum Associates, 1994.

Banner, David K., and T. Elaine Gagné. *Designing Effective Organizations: Traditional and Transformational Views.* Thousand Oaks, CA: Sage Publications, 1995.

Barnard, Chester I. *The Functions of the Executive.* Cambridge: Harvard University Press, 1938.

Barrick, Murray R., and Michael K. Mount. "The Big Five Personality Dimensions and Job Performance: A Meta-Analysis." *Personnel Psychology* 44, no. 1 (1991): 1–26.

Bass, Bernard M., and Ruth Bass. *The Bass Handbook of Leadership: Theory, Research, and Managerial Applications*, 4th ed. New York: The Free Press, 2008.

Beckhard, Richard, and Reuben T. Harris. *Organizational Transitions: Managing Complex Change*, 2nd edition. Reading, MA: Addison-Wesley Publishing Company, Inc., 1991.

Beckhard, Richard, and Wendy Pritchard. *Changing the Essence: The Art of Creating and Leading Fundamental Change in Organizations.* San Francisco: Jossey-Bass, 1992.

Beehr, Terry A. *Psychological Stress in the Workplace.* New York: Routledge, 1999.

Beer, Michael, and Anna Elise Walton. "Organizational Change and Development." In *Annual Review of Psychology*, vol. 38. Edited by Mark R. Rosenzweig and Lyman W. Porter. Stanford, CA: Annual Reviews, 1987, 339–367.

Blau, Peter M., and W. Richard Scott. *Formal Organizations.* San Francisco: Chandler Publishing Co., 1962.

Bond, Meg A., and Jean L. Pyle. "The Ecology of Diversity in Organizational Settings: Lessons from a Case Study." *Human Relations* 51, no. 5 (1998): 589–623.

Brandt, Richard B. *Ethical Theory: The Problems of Normative and Critical Ethics.* Englewood Cliffs, NJ: Prentice Hall, 1959.

Brodner, S. "The Movie That Changed My Life." *Premiere* (July 2002): 72.

Brown, L. David. *Managing Conflict at Organizational Interfaces*. Reading, MA: Addison-Wesley, 1983.

Buchholz, Rogene A. *Fundamental Concepts and Problems in Business Ethics*. Englewood Cliffs, NJ: Prentice Hall, 1989.

Burke, W. Warner. "Organization Change: What We Know, What We Need to Know." *Journal of Management Inquiry* 4, no. 2 (1995): 158–171.

Butler, Richard J. *Designing Organizations: A Decision-Making Perspective*. New York: Routledge, 1991.

Cairncross, Frances *The Death of Distance*. Boston: Harvard Business School Press, 1998.

Cartwright, Dorwin, and Alvin Frederick Zander. *Group Dynamics: Research and Theory*. New York: Harper & Row, Publishers, Inc., 1960.

Champoux, Joseph E. "Management Context of Not-for-Profit Organizations in the Next Millennium: Diversity, Quality, Technology, Global Environment, and Ethics." In *The Nonprofit Management Handbook*, 2d ed. 1999 supplement. Edited by Tracy D. Connors. New York: John Wiley & Sons, 1999, 7–9.

Champoux, Joseph E. "Seeing and Valuing Diversity Through Film." *Educational Media International* 36, no. 4 (1999): 310–316.

Champoux, Joseph E. "Animated Films as a Teaching Resource." *Journal of Management Education* 25, no. 1 (2001): 79–100.

Champoux, Joseph E. "European Films as a Management Education Teaching Resource." In *Changing the Way You Teach: Creative Tools for Management Educators*. Edited by T. Torres Coronas, M. Gascó Hernández, and A. Fernandes de Matos Coelho. Oviedo, Spain: Septem Ediciones, 2005, 85–106.

Champoux, Joseph E. *Organizational Behavior: Integrating Individuals, Groups, and Organizations*, 4e. New York: Taylor & Francis, 2011.

Clemens, John K., and Melora Wolff. *Movies to Manage by: Lessons in Leadership from Great Films*. Chicago: Contemporary Books, 1999.

Cooper, Cary L., Philip J. Dewe, and Michael P. O'Driscoll. *Organizational Stress: A Review and Critique of Theory, Research, and Applications*. Thousand Oaks, CA: Sage Publications, Inc., 2001.

Craddock, Jim, ed. *VideoHound's Golden Movie Retriever*. Farmington Hills, MI: Gale, Cengage Learning, 2014.

Culhane, Shamus. *Talking Animals and Other People*. New York: St. Martin's Press, 1986.

Davidoff, Jules B. *Differences in Visual Perception: The Individual Eye*. London: Crosby Lockwood Stapes, 1975.

Davis, B., and J. Calmes. "The House Passes Nafta–Trade Win: House Approves Nafta, Providing President With Crucial Victory." *The Wall Street Journal* (November 18, 1993): A1.

Davis, Margaret R., and David A. Weckler. *A Practical Guide to Organization Design*. Menlo Park, CA: Crisp Publications, 1996.

Deal, Terrence E., and Allan A. Kennedy. *Corporate Cultures: The Rites and Rituals of Corporate Life*. Reading, MA: Addison-Wesley, 1982.

Dember, William N. *Psychology of Perception*. New York: Holt, Rinehart and Winston, 1979.

Deutsch, Didier C. *VideoHound's Soundtracks: Music from the Movies, broadway and television*. Detroit, MI: Visible Ink Press, 1998.

Digman, John M. "Personality Structure: Emergence of the Five-Factor Model." *Annual Review of Psychology* 41 (1990): 417–440.

Duncan, Robert. "What Is the Right Organization Structure? Decision Tree Analysis Provides the Answer." *Organizational Dynamics* 7, no. 3 (1979): 447–461.

Etzioni, Amitai. *Modern Organizations*. Englewood Cliffs, NJ: Prentice Hall, 1964.

Evans, Martin G. "Organizational Behavior: The Central Role of Motivation." In *Yearly Review of Management of the Journal of Management*. Edited by Jerry G. Hunt and John D. Blair, 12, no. 2, 1986, 203–222.

Fairholm, Gilbert W. *Organizational Power Politics: Tactics in Organizational Leadership*. Santa Barbara, CA: Praeger, 2009.

Fairlamb, David. "Ready, Set, Euros!" *Business Week*. (July 2, 2001): 48–50.

Fields, Ronald, and Shaun O'L. Higgins. *Never Give a Sucker an Even Break: W. C. Fields on Business*. Paramus, NJ: Prentice Hall Press, 2000.

Fishbein, Martin, and Icek Ajzen. *Belief, Attitude, Intention and Behavior: An Introduction to Theory and Research*. Reading, MA: Addison-Wesley, 1975.

Fisher, C. "Organizational Socialization: An Integrative Review." In *Research in Personnel and Human Resource Management*, vol. 4. Edited by K. M. Rowland and G. R. Ferris. Greenwich, CT: JAI Press, 1986, 101–145.

Flamholtz, Eric G., and Yvonne Randle. *Changing the Game: Organizational Transformations of the First, Second, and Third Kinds*. New York: Oxford University Press, 1998.

Fowler, G. A. "Hollywood Ending: Stapler Becomes a Star." *The Wall Street Journal* (July 2, 2002): B1, B4.

Fox, Justin. "Europe Is Heading for a Wild Ride." *Fortune* (August 17, 1998): 145–146, 148–149.

Fox, Ken, Ed Grant, and Jo Imeson. *The Seventh Virgin Film Guide*. London: Virgin Books, 1998.

Garvin, David A. *Managing Quality: The Strategic and Competitive Edge*. New York: Free Press, 1988.

Gehani, R. Ray. "Quality Value-Chain: A Meta-Synthesis of Frontiers of Quality Movement." *Academy of Management Executive* 7, no. 2 (1993): 29–42.

Germain, D. 2002. "'Casablanca' Top Romance Film: Institute Picks 100 Best Love Stories." *The Associated Press*. As the story appeared in the *Albuquerque Journal*. (June 12, 2002): C13.

Glaser, Ronald, and Janice Kiecolt-Glaser. *Handbook of Human Stress and Immunity*. San Diego: Academic Press, 1994.

Goldhaber, Gerald M. *Organizational Communication*, 4th. Edition. Dubuque, IA: Wm. C. Brown, 1986.

Goldstone, Robert L. "Perceptual Learning." In *Annual Review of Psychology*, vol. 49, 585–612. Edited by Janet T. Spence, John M. Darley, and Donald J. Foss. Palo Alto: Annual Reviews, Inc., 1998.

Goodstein, Leonard D., and W. Warner Burke. "Creating Successful Organizational Change." *Organizational Dynamics* 19, no. 4 (1991): 5–17.

Graham, Lise, Leticia Peña, and Claudia Kocher, "*Other People's Money*: A Visual

Technology for Teaching Corporate Restructuring Cross-functionally." *Journal of Management Education* 23, no. 1 (1999): 53–64.

Green, Ronald N., and Aine Donovan. "The Methods of Business Ethics." In *The Oxford Handbook of Business Ethics*, chap. 1. Edited by George G. Brenkert, and Tom L. Beauchamp. New York: Oxford University Press, Inc., 2009.

Griener, Larry E., and Virginia E. Schein. *Power and Organization Development*. Reading, MA: Addison-Wesley, 1988.

Griffin, Ricky W. *Task Design: An Integrative Approach*. Glenview, IL: Scott, Foresman, 1982.

Gross, Neal, and Otis Port. "The Next WAVE." *Business Week* (August 31, 1998): 80, 82–83.

Hackman, J. Richard. "Work Design." In *Improving Life at Work: Behavioral Science Approaches to Organizational Change*, chap. 3. Edited by J. Richard Hackman and J. Lloyd Suttle. Santa Monica, CA: Goodyear Publishing Company, Inc., 1977.

Hackman, J. Richard, and Greg R. Oldham. *Work Redesign*. Reading, MA: Addison-Wesley, 1980.

Hare, A. Paul. *Groups, Teams, and Social Interaction: Theories and Applications*. New York: Praeger, 1992.

Hargrove, M. Blake, James C. Quick, Debra L. Nelson, and Jonathan D. Quick. "The Theory of Preventive Stress Management: A 33-year Review and Evaluation." *Stress and Health* 27, no. 3 (2011): 182–193.

Hayles, V. Robert, and Amida M. Russell. *The Diversity Directive: Why Some Initiatives Fail & What to Do About It*. Chicago: Irwin Professional Publishing, 1997.

Hempel, Jesse. "How Facebook Is Taking Over Our Lives." *Fortune* (March 2, 2009): 48–56.

Herzberg, Frederick. "One More Time: How Do You Motivate Employees?" *Harvard Business Review* 46 (January-February 1968): 53–62.

House, Robert J., and Ram N. Aditya. "The Social Scientific Study of Leadership: Quo Vadis?" *Journal of Management* 23, no. 3 (1997): 409–473.

House, Robert J., and Mary L. Baetz. "Leadership: Some Empirical Generalizations and New Research Directions." In *Research in Organizational Behavior*, vol. 1. Edited by Barry M. Staw. Greenwich, CT: JAI Press, 1979, 341–423.

Huber, George P. *Managerial Decision Making*. Glenview, IL: Scott, Foresman and Company, 1980.

Jackson, Susan E., and Associates, eds. *Diversity in the Workplace: Human Resources Initiatives*. New York: Guilford Press, 1992.

Jamieson, David, and Julie O'Mara. *Managing Workforce 2000: Gaining the Diversity Advantage*. San Francisco: Jossey-Bass, 1991.

Johnson, LouAnne. *My Posse Don't Do Homework*. New York: St. Martin's Press, 1993.

Johnston, William B. "Global Workforce 2000: The New Labor Market." *Harvard Business Review* 69, no. 2 (1991): 115–129.

Judge, Timothy A., and John D. Kammeyer-Mueller. "Job Attitudes." *Annual Review of Psychology* 63 (2012): 341–367.

Jurkiewicz, Kenneth "Using Film in the Humanities Classroom: The Case of *Metropolis*." *English Journal* 79, no. 3 (1990): 47–50.

Kanfer, Stefan. "*Serious Business: The Art and Commerce of Animation in America from Betty Boop to Toy Story.*" New York: Scribner, 1997.

Kanter, Rosabeth Moss. *Men and Women of the Corporation: New Edition.* New York: Basic Books, 1993.

Kirkland, Jr., R. I. "Entering a New Age of Boundless Competition." *Fortune* (March 14, 1988): 40–48.

Knapp, Mark L., Judith A. Hall, and Terrence G. Horgan. *Nonverbal Communication in Human Interaction*, 8th ed. Boston: Wadsworth, Cengage Learning, 2014.

Kramer, Michael W. *Organizational Socialization: Joining and Leaving Organizations.* Cambridge, UK: Polity Press, 2010.

Kranz, Gene. *Failure Is Not an Option: Mission Control from Mercury to Apollo 13 and Beyond.* New York: Simon & Shuster, Inc., 2000.

Lengnick-Hall, Cynthia A. "Customer Contributions to Quality: A Different View of the Customer-Oriented Firm." *Academy of Management Review* 21, no. 3 (1996): 791–824.

Levine, John M., and Richard L. Moreland. "Progress in Small Group Research." In *Annual Review of Psychology*, vol. 41, 585–634. Edited by Mark R. Rosensweig and Lyman W. Porter. Palo Alto, CA: Annual Reviews Inc., 1990.

Lyles, Marjorie A., and Ian I. Mitroff. 1980. "Organizational Problem Formulation: An Empirical Study." *Administrative Science Quarterly* 25, no. 1 (1980): 102–119.

Madison, Dan L., Robert W. Allen, Lyman W. Porter, Patricia A. Renwick, and Bronston T. Mayes. "Organizational Politics: An Exploration of Managers' Perceptions." *Human Relations* 33, no. 2 (1980): 79–100.

Maio, Gregory R., and Geoffrey Haddock. *The Psychology of Attitudes and Attitude Change.* London: SAGE Publications, Ltd., 2009.

Maltin, Leonard, ed. *Leonard Maltin's Movie Guide, 2015 Edition, The Modern Era.* New York: SIGNET, 2014.

Martin, Joanne. *Organizational Culture: Mapping the Terrain.* Thousand Oaks, CA: Sage Publications, Inc., 2002.

Maslow, Abraham H. "A Theory of Human Motivation." *Psychological Review* 50, no. 4 (1943): 370–396.

Maslow, Abraham H. (with Deborah C. Stephens and Gary Heil). *Maslow on Management.* New York: John Wiley & Sons, 1998.

Matteson, Michael T., and John M. Ivancevich. "Organizational Stressors and Heart Disease: A Research Model." *Academy of Management Review* 4, no. 3 (1979): 347–357.

Mayes, Bronston T., and Robert W. Allen. "Toward a Definition of Organizational Politics." *Academy of Management Journal* 2, no. 4 (1977): 635–644.

McCrae, Robert R., and Paul T. Costa Jr. "The Stability of Personality: Observations and Evaluations." *Current Directions in Psychological Science* 3, no. 6 (1994): 173–175.

McGuire, William J. "Attitudes and Attitude Change." In *Handbook of Social Psychology*, vol. I. Edited by Gardner Lindzey and Elliot Aronson. New York: Random House, 1985, 233–346.

Mintzberg, Henry. *Power In and Around Organizations.* Englewood Cliffs, NJ: Prentice Hall, 1983.

Mount, Michael K., Murray R. Barrick, and J. Perkins Strauss. "Validity of Observer

Ratings of the Big Five Personality Factors." *Journal of Applied Psychology* 72, no. 2 (1994): 272–280.

Nadler, David A., and Michael L. Tushman. *Competing by Design: The Power of Organizational Architecture.* New York: Oxford University Press, 1997.

Nowell-Smith, Geoffrey, ed. *The Oxford History of World Cinema.* Oxford: Oxford University Press, 1996.

Nutt, Paul C., and Robert W. Backoff. "Crafting Vision." *Journal of Management Inquiry* 6, no. 4 (1997): 308–328.

Oldham, Greg R. "Job Design." In *International Review of Industrial and Organizational Psychology*, chap. 2. Edited by Cary L. Cooper and Ivan T. Robertson. Chichester, England: John Wiley & Sons, Ltd., 1996.

Ostry, Sylvia. "Governments and Corporations in a Shrinking World: Trade and Innovation Policies in the United States, Europe, and Japan." *Columbia Journal of World Business* 25, no. 1/2 (1990): 10–16.

Ott, J. Steven. *The Organizational Culture Perspective.* Pacific Grove, CA: Brooks/Cole, 1989.

Pfeffer, Jeffrey. *Managing with Power: Politics and Influence in Organizations.* Boston: Harvard Business School Press, 1992.

Pinder, Craig C. *Work Motivation in Organizational Behavior*, 2e. Upper Saddle River, NJ: Prentice Hall, Inc., 2008.

Pondy, Louis R. "Organizational Conflict: Concepts and Models." *Administrative Science Quarterly* 12, no. 2 (1967): 296–320.

Porter, Lyman W., and Karlene H. Roberts. "Communication in Organizations." In *Handbook of Industrial and Organizational Psychology*, chap. 35. Edited by Marvin D. Dunnette. Chicago: Rand McNally College Pub. Co., 1976.

Pounds, W. E. "The Process of Problem Finding." *Industrial Management Review* 11, no. 1 (1969): 1–19.

Pruitt, Dean G., and Sung Hee Kim. *Social Conflict: Escalation, Stalemate, and Settlement*, 3rd. edition. New York: McGraw-Hill, 2004.

Quick, James C., and Jonathan D. Quick. *Organizational Stress and Preventive Management.* New York: McGraw-Hill, 1984.

Radford, G. S. *The Control of Quality in Manufacturing.* New York: The Ronald Press Company, 1922.

Robbins, Steven P. *Managing Organizational Conflict.* Englewood Cliffs, NJ: Prentice Hall, 1974.

Salancik, Gerald R., and Jeffrey Pfeffer. "Who Gets Power — And How They Hold Onto It: A Strategic Contingency Model of Power." *Organizational Dynamics* 5, no. 3 (1977): 3–21.

Schein, Edgar H. "Coming to a New Awareness of Organizational Culture." *Sloan Management Review* 25, no. 1 (1984): 3–16.

Schein, Edgar H. *Organizational Culture and Leadership.* 4th ed. San Francisco: Jossey-Bass, 2010.

Schneider, Benjamin, Mark G. Ehrhart, and William H. Macey. 2013. Organizational Climate and Culture. *Annual Review of Psychology.* 64 (2013): 361–388.

Scott, W. Richard. "Theory of Organizations." In *Handbook of Modern Sociology*. Edited by Robert E. L. Faris. Chicago: Rand McNally, 1964, 485–529.

Selye, Hans. "The Stress Concept: Past, Present, and Future." In *Stress Research*. Edited by Cary L. Cooper. New York: John Wiley & Sons, 1983, 1–19.

Shannon, Claude Elwood, Warren Weaver, Richard E. Blahut, and Bruce Hajek. *The Mathematical Theory of Communication*. Urbana, IL: University of Illinois Press, 1998.

Sheppard, Harold L., and Neal Q. Herrick. *Where Have All the Robots Gone?* New York: Free Press, 1972.

Snyder, Mark, and William Ickes. "Personality and Social Behavior." In *Handbook of Social Psychology*, vol. 2. Edited by Gardner Lindzey and Elliot Aronson. New York: Random House, 1985, 883–947.

Tjosvold, Dean. *The Conflict-Positive Organization: Stimulate Diversity and Create Unity*. Reading, MA: Addison-Wesley Longman, 1991.

Toossi, Mitra. "Labor force projections to 2022: the labor force participation rate continues to fall." *Monthly Labor Review*. 136, no. 1 (2013): 1–28.

Trice, Harrison Miller, and Janice M. Beyer. *The Cultures of Work Organizations*. Englewood Cliffs, NJ: Prentice Hall, 1993.

Van Maanen, John, and Edgar H. Schein. "Career Development." In *Improving Life at Work: Behavioral Science Approaches to Organizational Change*, chap. 2. Edited by J. Richard Hackman and J. Lloyd Suttle. Santa Monica: CA: Goodyear Publishing Company, 1977.

Van Maanen, John, and Edgar H. Schein. "Toward a Theory of Organizational Socialization." In *Research in Organizational Behavior*, vol. 1. Edited by Barry M. Staw and Larry L. Cummings. Greenwich, CT: JAI Press, 1979, 209–264.

Vecchiarelli, N. "Geek Chic." *Premiere*. (April 2002): 23–24.

Walker, Charles R., and Robert Guest. *The Man on the Assembly Line*. Cambridge, MA: Harvard University Press, 1952.

Wanberg, Connie R., ed. *The Oxford Handbook of Organizational Socialization*. New York: Oxford University Press, Inc., 2012.

Weiner, Bernard. *Human Motivation: Metaphors, Theories, and Research*. Newbury Park, CA: Sage Publications, 1992.

White, Karol K. *Understanding the Company Organization Chart*. New York: American Management Association, 1963.

Wiggins, Jerry S., and Aaron L. Pincus. "Personality: Structure and Assessment." In *Annual Review of Psychology*, vol. 43. Edited by Mark R. Rosensweig, and Lyman W. Porter. Stanford, CA: Annual Reviews, 1992, 473–504.

Wilson, Charles Z., and Marcus Alexis. "Basic Frameworks for Decisions." *Academy of Management Journal 5*, no. 2 (1962): 150–164.

Wood, Donna J. "Corporate Social Performance Revisited." *Academy of Management Review* 16, no. 4 (1991): 691–718.